Editor
Eric Migliaccio

Editor in Chief
Karen J. Goldfluss, M.S. Ed.

Creative Director
Sarah M. Smith

Cover Artist
Barb Lorseyedi
Marilyn Goldberg

Illustrator
Mark Mason

Art Coordinator
Renée Mc Elwee

Imaging
James Edward Grace
Craig Gunnell

Publisher
Mary D. Smith, M.S. Ed.

Author
Karen McRae

Teacher Created Resources
12621 Western Avenue
Garden Grove, CA 92841
www.teachercreated.com
ISBN: 978-1-4206-3967-4

Reprinted, 2026
Made in U.S.A.

Teacher Created Resources

Table of Contents

Table of Contents *(cont.)*

The goal of this book is to introduce and explore science concepts while also improving students' reading and comprehension skills. *Daily Warm-Ups: Science* contains a variety of passages to be read on a daily basis. Each passage is followed by comprehension questions and/or activities designed to deepen students' understanding of an important science concept.

How to Use this Book

In total, this book contains 160 warm-ups. Each 1-page warm-up introduces a unique science concept. The topics covered in this book fit into three categories:

Life Science **Physical Science** **Earth & Space Science**

The warm-ups in this book are divided into units, each of which explores an important scientific category. These units do not need to be done in the order in which they appear in the book. At any point, you may choose to skip ahead to a unit that covers a desired category. In addition, the warm-ups within each unit can be done in any order. Each page is a lesson on its own; students do not need information from one page to complete another. While this is true, the first page of each unit is usually an overview page that contains a lot of general information about the topic, and the last page of each unit is always a "Word Study" page that focuses on vocabulary related to the topic.

With the exception of the "Word Study" pages, there are two components to each warm-up:

1. **Reading Passage**
   With the implementation of Common Core State Standards, there has been an increased emphasis on reading more demanding text and on the inclusion of close reading to improve comprehension. Using short texts can be a helpful way to approach this goal, especially when dealing with a wide range of reading levels among students. In addition, many of the warm-ups in this book contain texts with varying structures. The use of charts, graphs, lists, and illustrations creates a higher level of text complexity. In doing so, this book provides students with more of the tools they need to practice close reading.
2. **Comprehension Questions and Activities**
   It is through the comprehension questions and activities included in each warm-up that students are able to respond to the reading passage. This book includes questions and activities that span the spectrum from literal to inferential to applied. **Literal questions** are those that can be answered directly from the text. **Inferential questions** are those that require the reader to think more deeply about what has been read. **Applied questions** challenge students to think even further about the text and incorporate personal experiences and knowledge into their responses.

In summary, these warm-ups provide students with an interesting, imaginative, and creative introduction to the many facets of science learning across the three basic areas of science instruction. They offer a taste of the diversity and complexity of science as a field of study, all while sharpening students' reading-comprehension skills.

Extras

- See pages 5–6 for a list of the Common Core State Standards met by the activities in this book.
- See pages 167–176 for a thorough and comprehensive answer key.

Common Core State Standards

The lessons and activities included in *Daily Warm-Ups: Science, Grade 2* meet one or more of the following Common Core State Standards. (©Copyright 2010. National Governors Association Center for Best Practices and Council of Chief State School Officers. All right reserved.) For more information about the Common Core State Standards, go to *http://www.corestandards.org/* or visit *http://www.teachercreated.com/standards/*.

Informational Text Standards	
Key Ideas and Details	**Units**
ELA.RI.2.1 Ask and answer such questions as *who, what, where, when, why*, and *how* to demonstrate understanding of key details in a text.	1–19
ELA.RI.2.2 Identify the main topic of a multiparagraph text as well as the focus of specific paragraphs within the text.	5, 15, 17, 18
ELA.RI.2.3 Describe the connection between a series of historical events, scientific ideas or concepts, or steps in technical procedures in a text.	3, 7, 8, 10, 15, 17, 18
Craft and Structure	**Units**
ELA.RI.2.4 Determine the meaning of words and phrases in a text relevant to a *grade 2 topic or subject area.*	1–19
ELA.RI.2.6 Identify the main purpose of a text, including what the author wants to answer, explain, or describe.	1–19
Integration of Knowledge and Ideas	**Units**
ELA.RI.2.8 Describe how reasons support specific points the author makes in a text.	5, 7, 11, 13, 14, 15, 18
Range of Reading and Level of Text Complexity	**Units**
ELA.RI.2.10 By the end of the year, read and comprehend informational texts, including history/social studies, science, and technical texts, in the grades 2–3 text complexity band proficiently, with scaffolding as needed at the high end of the range.	1–19

Foundational Skills	
Phonics and Word Recognition	**Units**
ELA.RF.2.3 Know and apply grade-level phonics and word-analysis skills in decoding words.	1–19
Fluency	**Units**
ELA.RF.2.4 Read with sufficient accuracy and fluency to support comprehension.	1–19

Common Core State Standards *(cont.)*

Writing Standards	
Text Types and Purposes	**Units**
ELA.W.2.2 Write informative/explanatory texts in which they introduce a topic, use facts and definitions to develop points, and provide a concluding statement or section.	3, 4, 7, 10, 13, 14, 16
ELA.W.2.3 Write narratives in which they recount a well-elaborated event or short sequence of events, include details to describe actions, thoughts, and feelings, use temporal words to signal event order, and provide a sense of closure.	1, 10
Research to Build and Present Knowledge	**Units**
ELA.W.2.8 Recall information from experiences or gather information from provided sources to answer a question.	1, 3, 6–8, 10–19

Language Standards	
Conventions of Standard English	**Units**
ELA.L.2.1 Demonstrate command of the conventions of standard English grammar and usage when writing or speaking.	1–19
ELA.L.2.2 Demonstrate command of the conventions of standard English capitalization, punctuation, and spelling when writing.	1–19
Knowledge of Language	**Units**
ELA.L.2.3 Use knowledge of language and its conventions when writing, speaking, reading, or listening.	1–19
Vocabulary Acquisition and Use	**Units**
ELA.L.2.4 Determine or clarify the meaning of unknown and multiple-meaning words and phrases based on grade 2 reading and content, choosing flexibly from a range of strategies.	1–19
ELA.L.2.5 Demonstrate understanding of word relationships and nuances in word meanings.	1–19

The World of the Living

Name: ______________________________

Many things are living. People are living. Animals and insects are living. So are trees and plants. Living things have a life cycle. This means that they are born, they grow, and they die. Living things use energy, like food or sunlight.

Living things come in all sizes. Some are very large. Blue whales can be almost 100 feet long. Redwood trees can grow to be 300 feet tall. Other living things are very small. Some are so small that they can only be seen with a microscope. Bacteria are living things that are too small to see with just your eyes.

What Did You Learn ?

1. Which of these is a living thing?

- Ⓐ grass
- Ⓑ water
- Ⓒ gasoline
- Ⓓ lawn mower

2. Which is **not** true about all living things?

- Ⓐ They use energy.
- Ⓑ They can walk.
- Ⓒ They are born.
- Ⓓ They have life cycles.

3. Bacteria

- Ⓐ are very small.
- Ⓑ have a life cycle.
- Ⓒ can only be seen with a microscope.
- Ⓓ Answers A, B, and C are correct.

For the next two questions, use the **greater than (>)** or **less than (<)** signs to show which living thing is longer.

4. a redwood tree ◯ a blue whale

5. bacteria ◯ a snail

Warm-Up 2

Separate the Living from the Non-Living

Name: ______________________________

Living things are born and they grow. Non-living things do not.

Directions: Can you find 5 living things and 5 non-living things in the word search? Circle each thing you find. Write each thing in the correct column below the word search. The first one has been done for you.

Hints:

- The living things are written **across** in the word search.
- The non-living things are written **up and down** in the word search.

P	C	C	M	U	C	Z	O	W	L
O	A	L	J	Q	O	R	S	T	U
F	R	O	G	L	M	P	Y	D	U
L	V	C	S	S	P	I	D	E	R
E	A	K	K	L	U	Z	Z	S	A
P	P	L	A	N	T	Z	E	K	V
W	M	M	O	Q	E	A	U	N	G
A	G	R	Y	T	R	E	E	J	A

Living Things	Non-Living Things
____________	clock
____________	____________
____________	____________
____________	____________
____________	____________
____________	____________

A Walk in the Park

Warm-Up 3

Name: ________________________________

Directions: Take a look at the picture below. Can you find the things that are living?

- Draw a **circle** around the things that are living.
- Draw an **X** on the things that are not living.

Warm-Up 4

The Life Cycle of a Ladybug

Name: ____________________________________

Living things have a life cycle. They are born, and they go through changes.

Directions: A ladybug goes through four main stages. Read about each stage. Then, label and color the picture below. Use the words from the box to the right.

Ladybug Words	
eggs	larva
pupa	adult

- **The 1st Stage:** Ladybug babies hatch from **eggs**. Ladybug mothers lay their eggs on the undersides of leaves. This protects them from being seen. The eggs look like pale-yellow jellybeans.
- **The 2nd Stage:** When an egg hatches, a baby ladybug comes out. It is called a **larva**. A ladybug larva is black with orange marks on its back. As it grows, it sheds its skin. It does this many times.
- **The 3rd Stage:** Now the larva becomes a **pupa**. The pupa attaches itself to a leaf and stays there. The pupa is covered in a bright-yellow skin. It begins changing beneath that skin.
- **The 4th Stage:** Once it has completely changed, the larva's skin splits open. The **adult** ladybug comes out. Its shell is soft and pink. The shell hardens after a few hours. It becomes bright red with black spots.

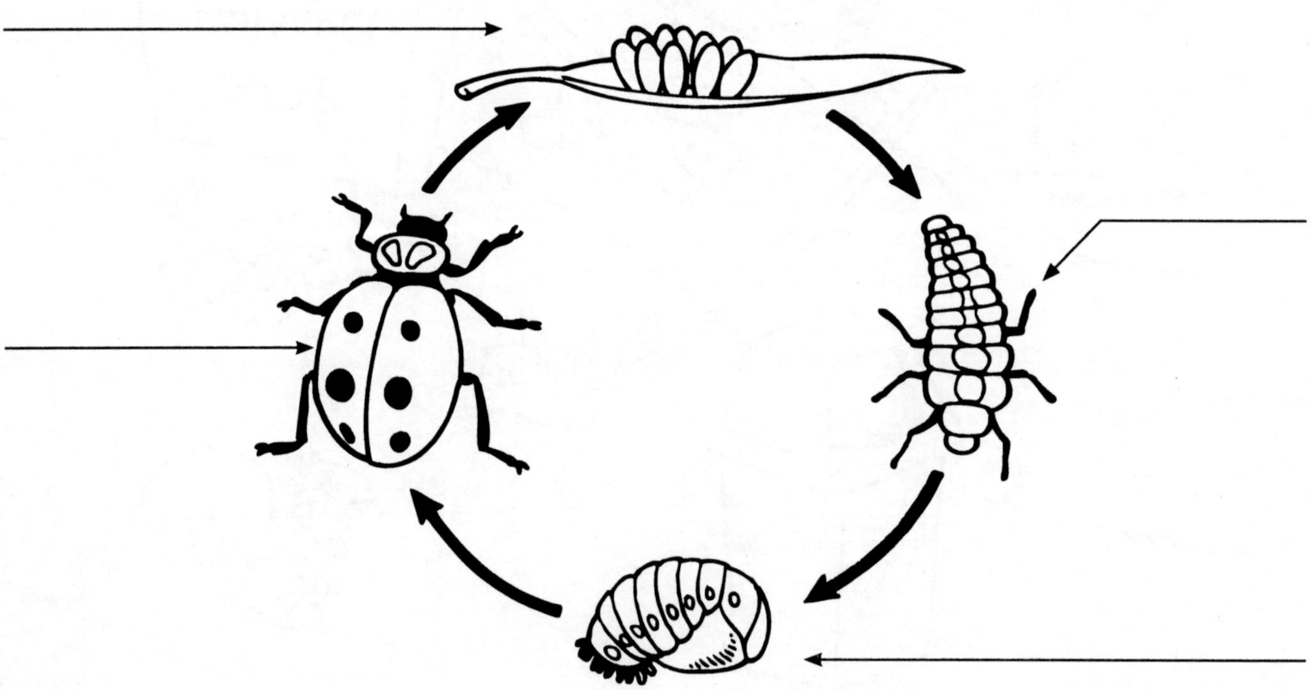

The Creature That Does Not Die

Warm-Up 5

Name: ______________________________

Living things have life cycles. This means that they are born, they live and grow, and then they die. However, scientists have found an animal that seems to not die. This animal can stop the cycle. It can start the cycle over again. This animal is called the immortal jellyfish.

The word *immortal* means "lives forever" or "does not die." When this unique creature reaches a certain age, it can change itself back. It can become like it was when it was younger. It might be able to do this forever. Scientists think this may be possible.

Immortal Jellyfish

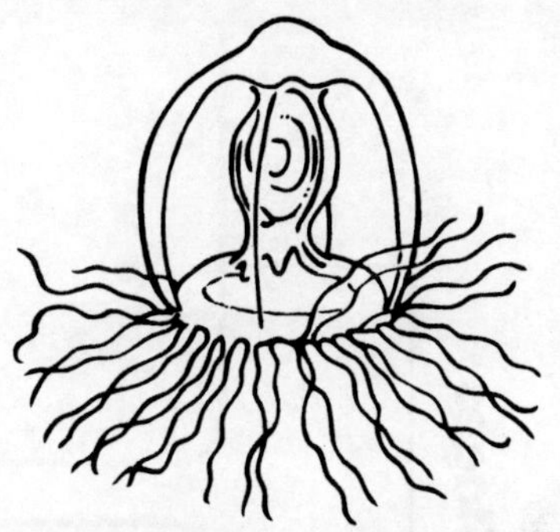

Directions: Write a short story about an immortal jellyfish. Give the jellyfish a friend that is another type of animal. That other animal is not immortal. Have the jellyfish and its friend talk about their lives. Use the back of the page if you need more room to write.

Unit 1 — Life Science: Living Things

Warm-Up 6

The Stages of Your Life

Name: ______________________________

Living things change as they grow, but they don't all change and grow in the same way. Even people go through stages at different times than other people.

Directions: Think about your own life cycle. Draw two pictures showing the stages of life you have already gone through. Then, draw two stages of life you will go through in the future. Next to each picture, write one sentence about that stage of life.

Past Stages

Future Stages

Match the Parents with Their Children

Warm-Up 7

Name: ____

Think about how animals are born and how they grow. Some hatch from an egg. Others do not. Some babies look very much like their parents. Some babies look very different from their parents when they are young.

Directions: Look at each baby on the left. Draw a line to match it with its parent on the right.

1. 

a. 

2. 

b. 

3. 

c. 

4. 

d. 

5. 

e. 

6. Which three babies look the most like their parents?

______________________ ______________________ ______________________

7. Which two babies look the least like their parents?

______________________ ______________________

Warm-Up 8

Passed Down from Your Parents

Name: ______________________________

What color eyes do you have? Do your parents have the same color eyes? People and other animals inherit traits like eye color from their parents. To inherit something is to have it passed down to you from your parents. Eye color is just one of the many traits you inherited from your parents.

Not all traits are inherited. Some traits you are not born with. You are not born with good manners or the ability to read, for example. You learn these things. Having good manners is a learned trait.

Part 1 Directions: Read each trait below. If it is a trait you could **inherit** from your parents, write **I** next to it. If it is a trait that is **learned**, write **L**.

_______ **1.** having big feet

_______ **2.** being polite

_______ **3.** liking video games

_______ **4.** being shy

_______ **5.** having naturally curly hair

_______ **6.** being a good swimmer

_______ **7.** being short or tall

_______ **8.** having small eyes

_______ **9.** having long arms

_______ **10.** having a positive attitude

Part 2 Directions: Now think about yourself. List three traits of yours that you inherited from your parents. List three traits that you have learned.

Inherited Traits

1. ______________________________

2. ______________________________

3. ______________________________

Learned Traits

1. ______________________________

2. ______________________________

3. ______________________________

Warm-Up 9

Name: ____

Part 1 Directions: All of the things listed in the box below are living things. Which type of living thing is each one? Put each one in the correct category.

Hint: Each living thing in the box has the same number of syllables as the category to which it belongs.

beetle	gorilla	moss
cricket	halibut	oak
crocodile	locust	pelican
elephant	mantis	pine
fern	mint	termite

Plants	**Insects**	**Vertebrates** (animals with backbones)
1 syllable	*2 syllables*	*3 syllables*
____________	____________	____________
____________	____________	____________
____________	____________	____________
____________	____________	____________
____________	____________	____________

Part 2 Directions: Can you think of more living things? Write some under each of these categories.

Plants	**Insects**	**Vertebrates**
____________	____________	____________
____________	____________	____________
____________	____________	____________

Warm-Up 10

A Place to Live and Grow

Name: ______________________________

Living things need a place to live. They need a place where they can find food. They need a place that has the right kind of climate, or weather. They need a place where they can be safe. They need a good **environment**.

The perfect environment for one living thing might not be good for another. Some animals can only live on land, for example. Others, like dolphins and fish, must live in the water. Animals that are lightweight and good climbers can live high up in trees. Some animals have thick coats of fur or thick layers of fat that allow them to live in cold places. Other animals, such as camels, can go a long time without drinking water. This is why they can live in hot, dry deserts. There are plants like this, too. A cactus is good at storing water, and it only needs to use a little bit at a time to survive. Other plants, such as seaweed, only grow in water.

Food is a very important part of a living thing's environment. Many plants need to be in a place where they get a lot of sunlight. Sunlight helps them make their own food. Animals need to live in places where water and food can be found. Even people do this. Most people live near places where food is grown or can be bought. Most people live where there is plenty of water to drink.

What Did You Learn ?

1. What is part of an animal's environment?

Ⓐ a place to get food
Ⓑ a place to grow
Ⓒ a place to be safe
Ⓓ All of the answers are correct.

2. Which of these animals could **not** live in a tree?

Ⓐ squirrel
Ⓑ snake
Ⓒ zebra
Ⓓ monkey

3. A cactus only needs a little water to survive. In that way, which of these animals is most like a cactus?

Ⓐ goldfish
Ⓑ camel
Ⓒ dog
Ⓓ dolphin

What Am I ?

Plants need me to help them make their own food. I am . . .

s ___ n l ___ ___ ___ ___.

Animals and Their Habitats

Name: ______________________________

A *habitat* is a place where a type of animal lives. A habitat has all the things that an animal needs. A habitat is more than a home. It is the weather, the food, and the protection a place has to offer an animal.

Directions: Look at the habitats drawn below. Choose one animal from the **Animals** box. Draw that animal in its habitat. Write the name of the animal on the line.

Animals	
camel	crocodile
monkey	whale

1. ocean

____

2. desert

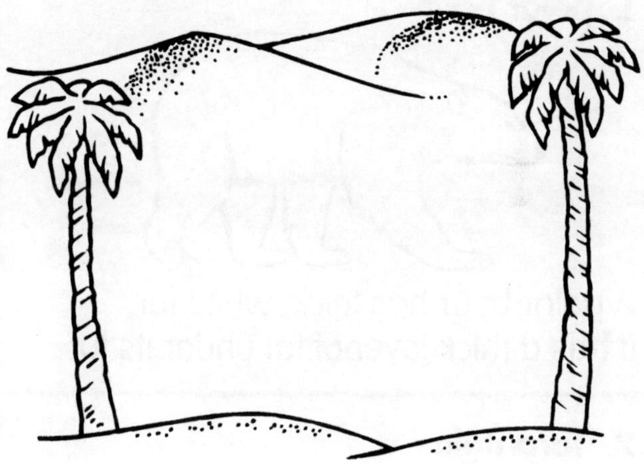

____

3. swamp

____

4. jungle

____

Warm-Up 12

Finding Just the Right Place

Name: ______________________________

Some living things need just the right place to live and grow. Look at these places:

- **Place A** is warm. It has lots of green plants.
- **Place B** is very cold. There is a lot of snow in this place.
- **Place C** is hot and sunny. The land here is mostly flat dirt.

Directions: Now read about three different animals. Think about them. Which place would they like to live in? Circle your answer.

---

1. polar bear

A polar bear has thick, white fur.
It has a thick layer of fat under its fur.

(circle one)

Place A

Place B

Place C

---

2. tarantula

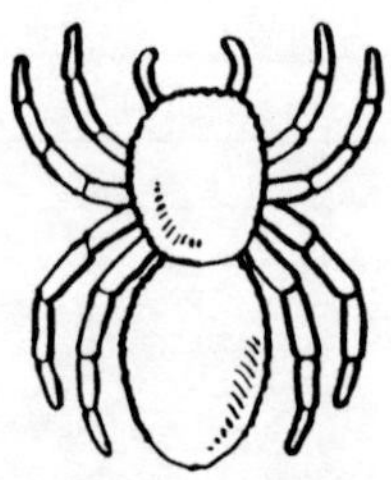

A tarantula hunts at night.
It lives in a hole that it makes in the ground.

(circle one)

Place A

Place B

Place C

---

3. toucan

A toucan lives in a hole in a tree.
It has short wings, and it can't fly far.

(circle one)

Place A

Place B

Place C

Warm-Up 13

Warm and Wet and Full of Life

Name: ______________________________

There are millions of different species (types) of plants and animals in the world. More than half of them live in tropical rainforests. Tropical rainforests are warm and wet and full of life.

There are different layers to tropical rainforests. The very top layer is called the **emergent layer**. The very tallest trees form this layer. It is hot and windy. Eagles and bats live there.

The next layer is called the **canopy layer**. Very large trees make up this layer. Here you can find about 50% of all the species of plants and 25% of all the species of insects in the world.

The **understory layer** is the area between the canopy and the ground. Birds, snakes, lizards, and leopards live in this section.

The **forest floor** is at the bottom of the rainforest. Not much sunlight reaches this layer. Only certain plants can grow down on the forest floor.

Directions: The picture below shows the different layers of the rainforest. Draw lines to match the names on the left to the layers shown in the picture. The first one has been done for you. Then, circle the layer on the picture where most snakes and lizards live.

canopy layer

emergent layer

forest floor

understory layer

Warm-Up 14

Some Like It Hot, and Here's Why

Name: ______________________________

Deserts are hot. Water is hard to find. Sand blows into your eyes, ears, and nose. Who would want to live there?

Camels live in the desert. It is the perfect place for them. They can go a week without drinking water. Their bodies are made for the hot, dry desert.

Directions: Look at the picture of the camel. The names of its body parts are all scrambled up! Unscramble the letters to name the parts that allow it to love the desert. (**Hint:** The first letter in each word is darker than the others.)

1. The camel's ____ ____ ____ ____ ____ store fat, which can be used for water and energy. Some camels have one. Some have two.

2. The camel's ____ ____ ____ ____ reflects sunlight. A camel doesn't sweat until its body temperature is 107°F. You lose water when you sweat.

3. The camel's blood ____ ____ ____ ____ ____ are a different shape than those of other mammals. This helps blood flow without much water.

4. The camel's ____ ____ ____ ____ ____ ____ ____ ____ can open and close. The camel closes them to keep sand out of its nose.

5. The camel's ____ ____ ____ ____ ____ ____ are long. They keep sand from blowing into its eyes.

When the Weather Turns Cold

Warm-Up 15

Name: ______________________________

Animals have to protect themselves from cold weather. Some have thick fur. Some have an extra layer of fat to keep them warm. Some animals must hibernate. When an animal hibernates, it slows its body down. It breathes less. Its heart beats less. It stays in one place and eats very little food.

Chipmunks are animals that hibernate. They start getting ready in the summer. First, they eat extra food. This fattens them up. They also start storing extra seeds and nuts in their homes under the ground. This will give them food to eat during the winter.

When winter begins, chipmunks dig deep down into their homes. They then let their bodies slow way down. Their hearts slow down. Their breathing does, too. Their body temperature drops down. They stay very still. It is almost as if they are asleep for many days. By doing these things, chipmunks need less food to survive. Their bodies live off of the extra food they ate at the end of the summer. Once in a while, the chipmunks wake up, eat some seeds and nuts, and then go back to sleep. When the weather gets warmer, chipmunks stop hibernating completely. Male chipmunks wake up first.

Directions: Put the parts of the hibernation process in order from **1** to **5**. Put a **1** by the thing that happens first. Put a **5** by the thing that happens last.

_______ The chipmunk's heartbeat and breathing slow down.

_______ The female chipmunk stops hibernating.

_______ The chipmunk stores extra food in its home.

_______ The male chipmunk stops hibernating.

_______ The chipmunk digs deep down into its home.

Warm-Up 16

What's for Dinner?

Name: ______________________________

Food is an important part of life. Food gives energy to living things. Plants can use sunlight to make their own food. Animals need to eat things.

- Some animals just eat plants. These animals are called **herbivores**.
- Some only eat other animals. These animals are called **carnivores**.
- Some animals eat both plants *and* animals. They are called **omnivores**.

Directions: Look at each animal. Read about some of its favorite things to eat. Write **H** (for **herbivore**), **C** (for **carnivore**), or **O** (for **omnivore**).

1. **Sharks** eat fish, squids, and seals.

____

2. **Bears** eat fish, acorns, and berries.

____

3. **Zebras** eat grasses, shrubs, and tree bark.

____

4. **Crows** eat nuts, worms, and eggs.

____

5. **Gorillas** eat fruits, leaves, and bamboo.

____

6. **Owls** eat insects, spiders, and snails.

____

Warm-Up 17

The Parts of a Food Chain

Name: ______________________________

Food is an important part of any environment where things live. Each living thing needs energy to live and grow. Most living things get their energy from food. One thing eats another. It is then eaten by another living thing. This is how the food chain works.

Think about these five living things. How are they all related to each other?

owls **snakes** **frogs** **caterpillars** **plant leaves**

These things are all part of one food chain. Owls eat snakes. Snakes eat frogs. Frogs eat caterpillars. Caterpillars munch on leaves from plants. What do plants eat? Plants don't need to eat. They get their energy directly from the sun.

Directions: Cut out the pictures below. Put them in the correct order to complete the food chain. Use the information from the story to help you.

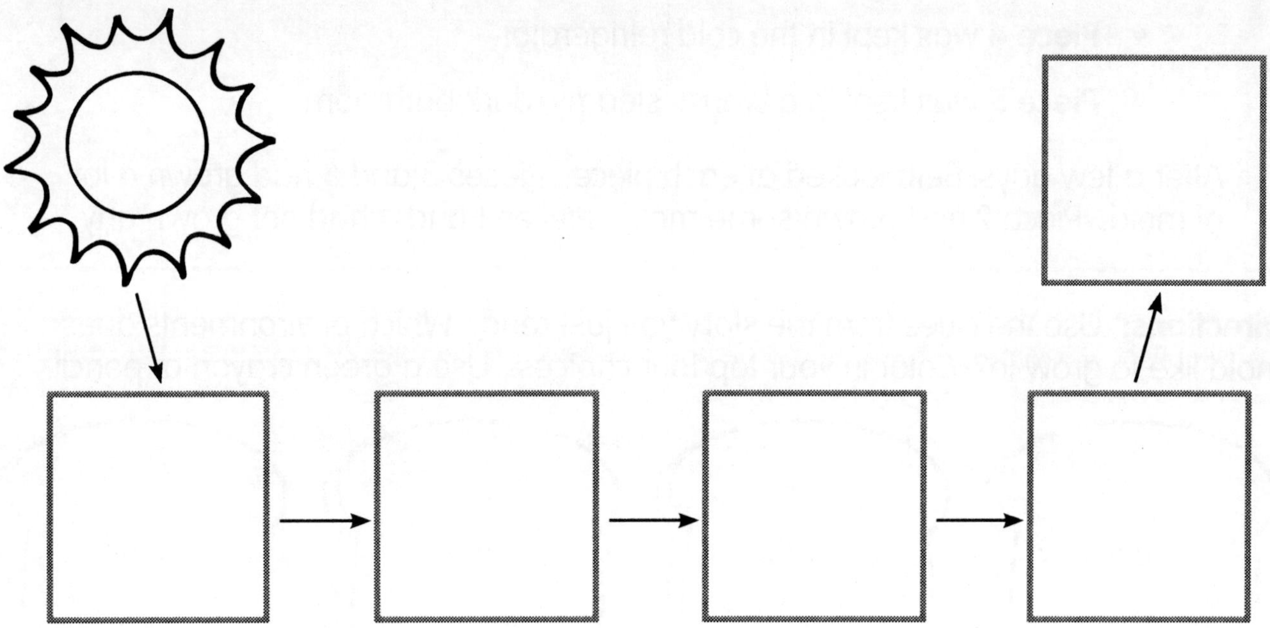

caterpillar **frog** **owl** **plant** **snake**

Warm-Up 18

It's Gross, It's Green, and It's Alive!

Name: ______________________________

Have you ever seen something green and furry growing on bread or fruit? That's mold, and you don't want to eat it. Mold is a type of fungus. It's alive, and there is a good reason why it grew on your food.

Mold is just like other living things: it lives and grows best in a certain environment.

Here is a story about mold:

> Beth wanted to see how mold grew on bread. She used five pieces of bread.
>
> - **Piece 1** was tightly wrapped in plastic and put in a well-lit place.
> - **Piece 2** was sitting on a dry plate in a dark place.
> - **Piece 3** was also sitting on a plate in a dark place. Beth put a few drops of water on it each day.
> - **Piece 4** was kept in the cold refrigerator.
> - **Piece 5** was kept in a warm, steamy, dark bathroom.
>
> After a few days, Beth looked at each piece. Pieces 3 and 5 had grown a lot of mold. Piece 2 had grown some mold. Pieces 1 and 4 had not grown any.

Directions: Use the clues from the story you just read. Which environments does mold like to grow in? Color in your top four choices. Use a green crayon or pencil.

Warm-Up 19

Name: ______________________________

Directions: Read the clues and complete the sentences. Choose from the words in the **Answers Box**.

Hint: Each clue has an underlined word that can help you answer the question.

Answers Box		
Antarctica	habitat	termites
box jellyfish	tapeworm	

1. Clue: Animals make it a habit to live in a place that fits their needs perfectly.

A place where an animal makes its home is called its

______________________________.

2. Clue: These mighty insects can build mounds that are up to 30 feet tall.

The small insects that work together to build tall mounds are called

______________________________.

3. Clue: Despite this continent's name, no ants live on it.

The only continent that is not home to ants is called

______________________________.

4. Clue: You could be in a real jam if you met up with this animal in the ocean.

One of the world's most venomous animals is a sea creature called the

______________________________.

5. Clue: This long, flat pest will really stick to the insides of other animals.

One animal that gets inside another animal and lives there is called the

______________________________.

Warm-Up 20

Insects Are Everywhere!

Name: ______________________________

Look just about anywhere, and you will see an insect. Insects make up more than half of the living things on Earth. They can live in almost any environment. Some very small insects even live in Antarctica. Antarctica is very cold and icy. Insects are everywhere!

Insects are cold-blooded, and most of them hatch from eggs. Most insects move about by walking or flying. Some can swim. Adult insects have three body parts and six legs. This is one reason why spiders, snails, and worms are not insects.

Most people look at insects as pests. Some insects are useful, though. We get silk from silkworms. (Silkworms are insects because they grow up to be moths!) Bees give us honey and help flowers grow. Some insects eat more dangerous insects.

What Did You Learn ?

1. Which is true about insects?
   - Ⓐ Most of them live in Antarctica.
   - Ⓑ Most of them can swim.
   - Ⓒ Most of them are spiders.
   - Ⓓ Most of them hatch from eggs.

2. Which is **not** true about some insects?
   - Ⓐ They have six legs.
   - Ⓑ They are warm-blooded.
   - Ⓒ They give us honey.
   - Ⓓ They live in cold places.

3. Only one of these pie charts *could be* correct. Which one?

Ⓐ

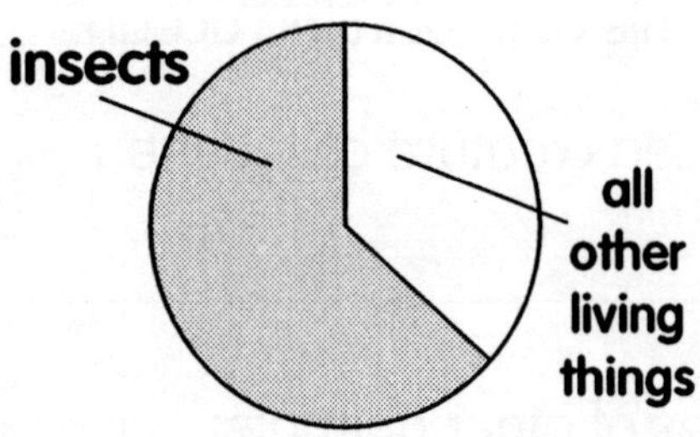

Ⓑ

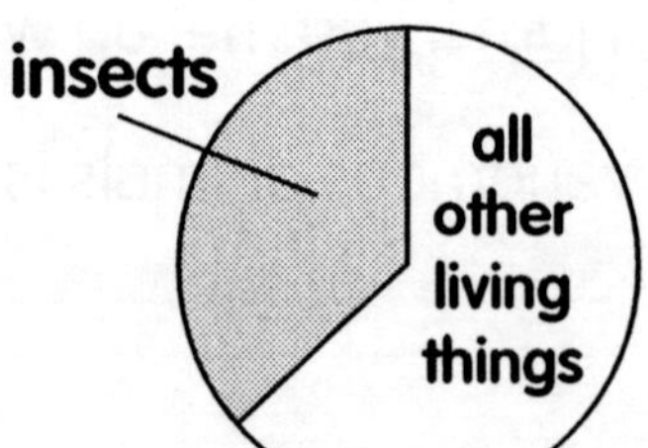

Ⓒ

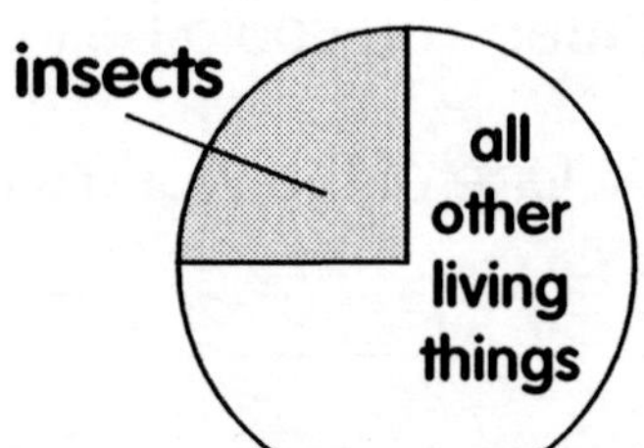

Explain your answer. ______________________________

____

Name: ____________________________________

Directions: Look at the picture. It doesn't look like much yet. It's missing things. Follow the instructions below to add parts to the picture. When you are finished, an insect will be staring back at you.

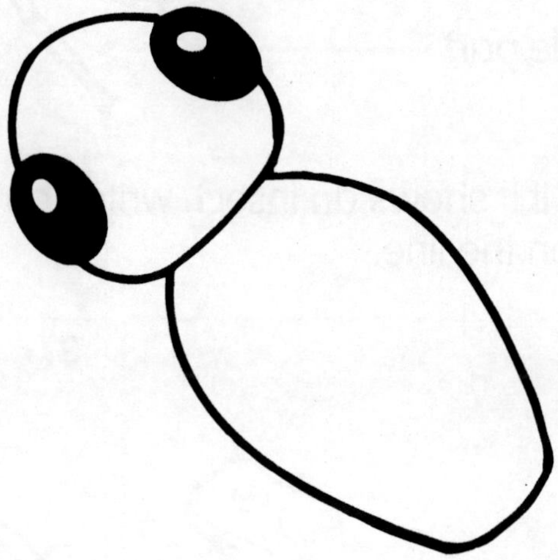

1. All insects have three body parts. Add an abdomen to the bottom of the drawing. It should be much larger than the other two parts.
2. All insects have six legs. They have three on each side. Add six legs to the thorax (middle part).
3. Many insects have wings. Add a wing to each side of the thorax.
4. An insect has two feelers called antennae on its head. Each feeler is very thin. Insects use these to smell, feel, and taste things. Add two antennae to the insect's head.

Warm-Up 22

Insect or Not?

Name: ______________________________

Not every creepy crawly is an insect. To be an insect, a creature must have . . .

- three body parts
- two antennae
- six legs attached to the middle part

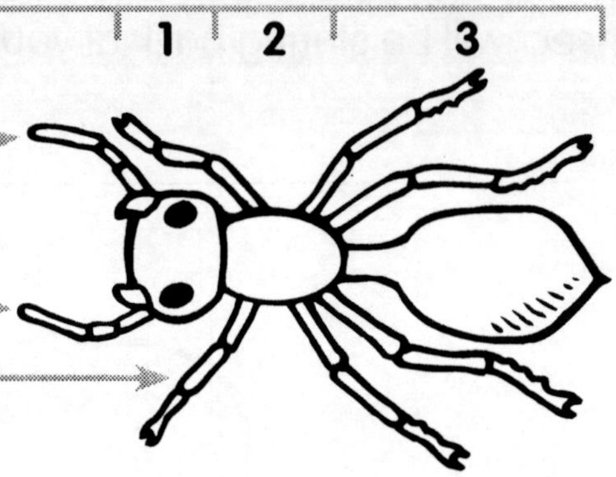

Directions: Look at each picture. If it shows an insect, write **I** on the line. If the creature is not an insect, write **N** on the line.

1.

____

2.

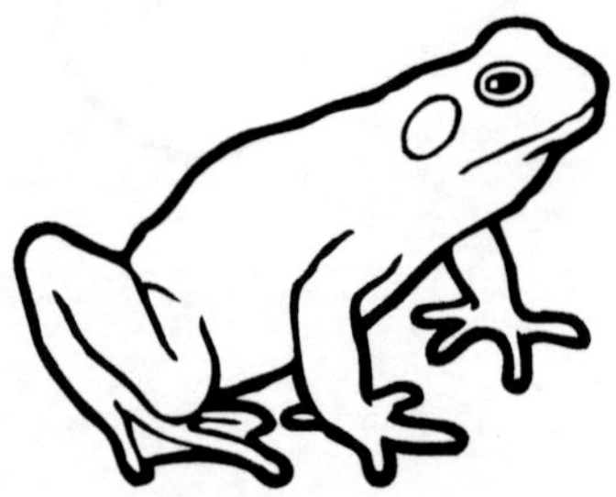

____

3.

____

4.

____

5.

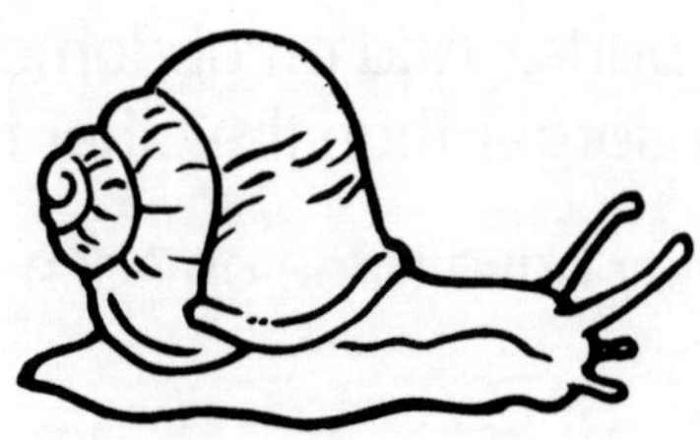

____

6.

____

Pets, Pests, or Snacks?

Name: ______________________________

Most people don't seem to like insects. They think insects are creepy, dirty, and downright disgusting. But did you know that some people eat bugs? Some people even keep them as pets. It's true!

Pets

Here are some insects that people keep as pets:

 ants

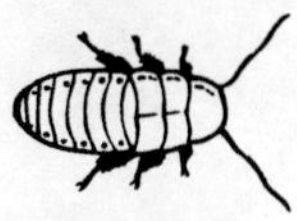 hissing cockroaches

 millipedes

 praying mantises

 tarantulas

Food

Here are some insects that people eat as food:

 cicadas

 crickets

 mealworms

 scorpions

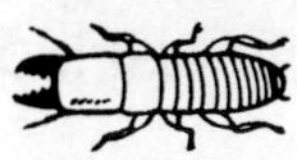 termites

Directions: Think about the following questions. Give your best answer.

1. Have you ever eaten an insect?

If **YES**, which one? How did it taste?

If **NO**, which one would you try? How do you think it would taste?

____

____

____

2. What insect would make the best pet? Explain your answer.

____

____

____

Warm-Up 24

A Job for Every Ant

Name: ______________________________

Ants are so small, but they can do so much. They can live well in almost any environment. They use the resources of the land to feed and defend themselves. What could be their secret to success? It's this: Ants are great at working together.

Ants live together in colonies. Some colonies are really large. There can be over 1 million ants living in a colony.

Each type of ant in the colony has a job to do:

- **Workers** — These small, female ants do a lot of jobs. They build the underground nest where ants live. They also bring food into the nest from outside.
- **Soldiers** — These female ants have larger heads and jaws than the worker ants. They protect the colony.
- **Drones** — Drones are the only male ants in the colony. They have wings. They do not live long.
- **Queen** — She is the founder and mother of the colony. She can give birth to thousands of eggs each day! And she can live over 25 years!

Directions: Use what you have just learned to answer these ant questions.

1. Write the names of the type of ants in the correct box. One has been written for you.

Male	Female
	workers

2. Draw lines to match each type of ant with its description.

drone	big jaws
queen	dies young
soldier	many jobs
worker	starts colony

Quick Quiz: I have the longest lifespan of any insect. I am a . . .

___ u ___ ___ ___   a ___ ___

Be as Busy as a Bee

Name: ______________________________________

Have you ever wondered how bees make honey? It takes a lot of work!

First, a bee visits a flower. The bee collects nectar from the flower. Nectar is like a mix of sugar and water. The bee takes that nectar and flies it back to the beehive. Other bees at the hive help take the nectar and store it in the hive. The bees help keep the nectar warm. They also beat their wings to move air across the nectar. This helps turn it into honey.

Directions: Can you help the bee find some nectar and get it back to her hive? Find the right path in the maze. First, find the way to the flower. Then, find the way to the hive.

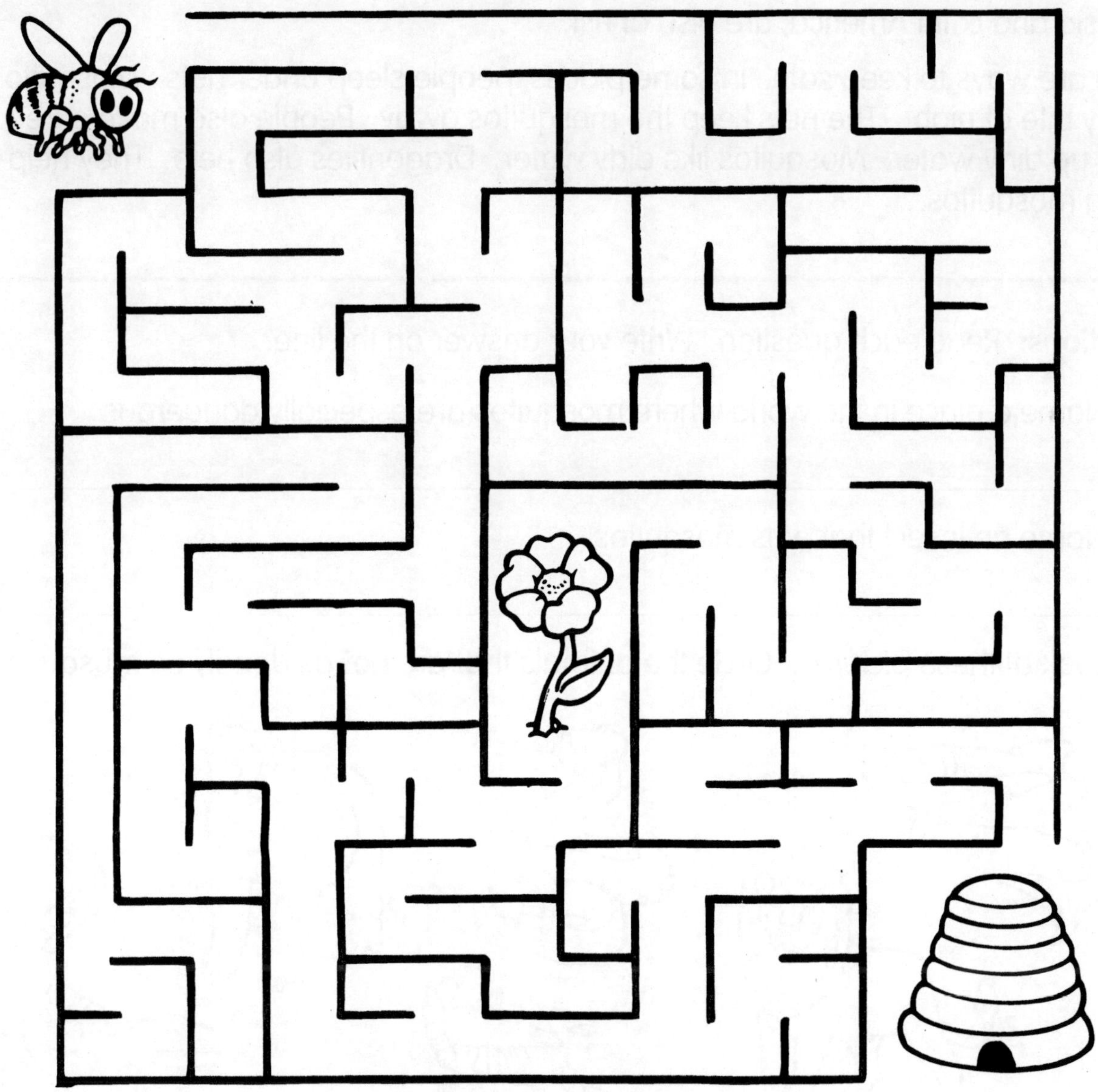

The Deadliest Animal on Earth

Name: ______________________________

Which animal is the deadliest to people? Make three guesses. Write the names of the three most dangerous animals you can think of.

______________ ______________ ______________

Did you guess "sharks"? Sharks are scary. But they kill fewer than 10 people each year. How about snakes? Crocodiles? Killer bees? Lions? None of these is correct. Mosquitos are the deadliest animals on Earth.

Mosquitos carry diseases. When they bite humans and other animals, they can give those diseases to the animals. Up to 2 million people die each year from diseases given to them by mosquitos. Many of these deaths happen in Africa. Other places, like Asia and Latin America, are also at risk.

There are ways to keep safe. In some places, people sleep under nets. Mosquitos mostly bite at night. The nets keep the mosquitos away. People also make sure to clean up dirty water. Mosquitos like dirty water. Dragonflies also help. They help by eating mosquitos.

Directions: Read each question. Write your answer on the line.

1. Name a place in the world where mosquitos are especially dangerous.

____

2. Name an insect that eats mosquitos.

____

3. Look at these pictures. Circle the animals that are **not** as deadly as mosquitos.

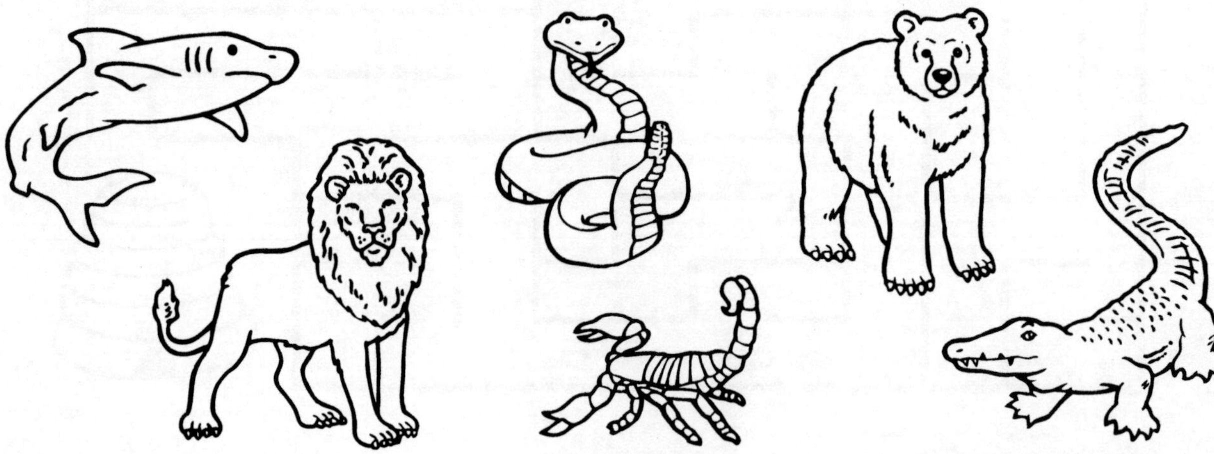

Word Study

Warm-Up 27

Name: ______________________________

Some words are made up of two smaller words joined together. These words are called **compound words**. *Baseball* and *flashlight* are two examples.

base + ball = baseball **flash + light = flashlight**

Part 1 Directions: Some insect names are compound words. Their names are made up of two smaller words. Draw a line to connect the first part of the word with the second part of the word. Then, draw a line to connect the second part of the word with the picture of the insect. The first one is done for you.

butter	**bug**	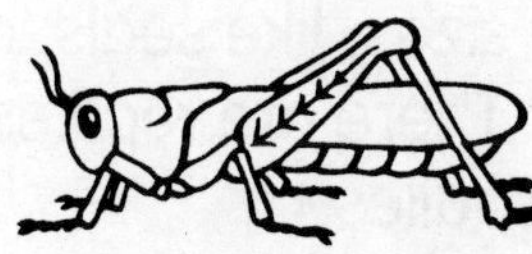
ear	**fly**	
grass	**hopper**	
lady	**wig**	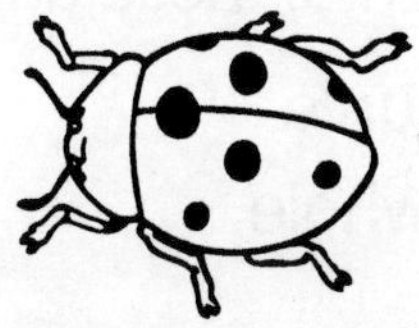
silk	**worm**	

Part 2 Directions: Choose one of the insect names from above. Why do you think the insect is named that? You can give an answer that you think is true, or you can make up a silly reason for the insect having that name.

____

____

____

____

Warm-Up 28

There Are Many Fish (and Other Animals) in the Sea

Name: ______________________________

Over 70 percent of Earth's surface is covered in water. Millions of different types of plants and animals live in the water. Think of just the animals. There are many kinds of fish, from tiny sardines to great white sharks. There are invertebrates, like jellyfish and squids. Invertebrates are animals that do not have backbones. There are mammals of many sizes, like seals, dolphins, and whales. There are reptiles, like turtles and crocodiles.

Not every underwater environment is the same. Some animals live in fresh water, such as in lakes and rivers. Many animals live in salt water, such as the ocean. Some animals live near the shore, while others live out in the open sea. Some animals live deep under the sea, where it is very cold and very dark.

What Did You Learn ?

1. How much of Earth's surface is **not** covered in water?

   Ⓐ over 70 percent

   Ⓑ about 70 percent

   Ⓒ under 30 percent

   Ⓓ over 30 percent

2. Which of these animals is **not** a mammal?

   Ⓐ turtle

   Ⓑ whale

   Ⓒ dolphin

   Ⓓ seal

3. Draw lines to match each sea creature to the type of animal it is.

crocodile	**fish**
shark	**invertebrate**
squid	**mammal**
whale	**reptile**

What Am I ?

I am the type of water found in the ocean.

___ ___ ___ ___   w a t e r

Water, Water All Around

Name: ______________________________

About 71% of Earth's surface is covered in water. That's a lot of water for animals to call home.

Part 1 Directions: Section A is 71% of the circle. Use a blue pencil or crayon to color section A on the circle below. Then, complete the sentence below.

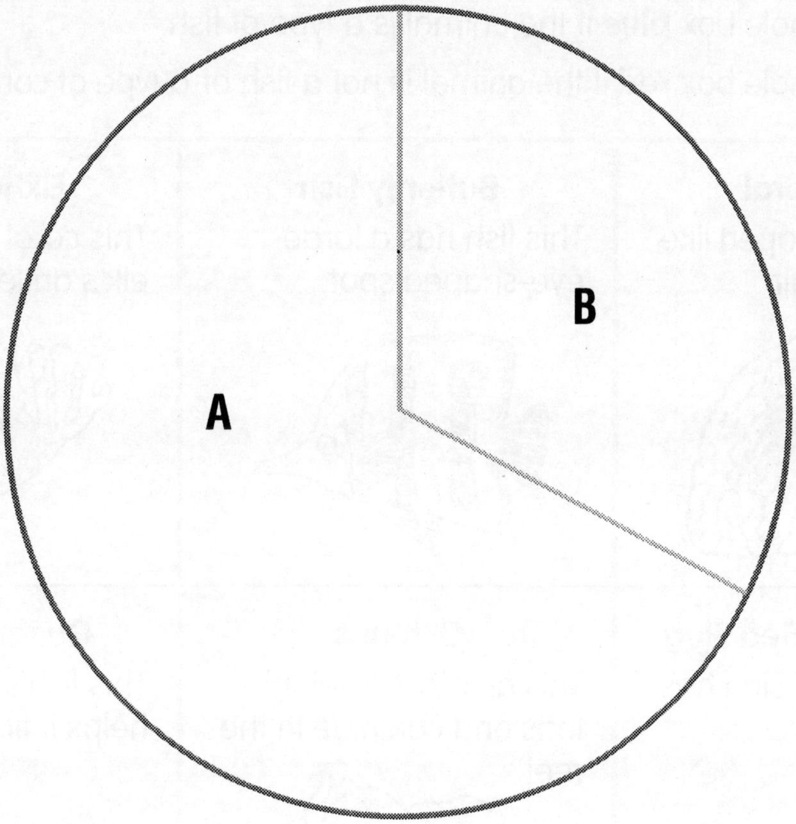

I colored ____________ of the circle above.

Ⓐ less than half   Ⓑ about half   Ⓒ more than half

Part 2 Directions: Cut out each animal and glue or tape it onto the circle. Put the animals that live in the water on the blue part of the circle. Put the animals that live on land on the other part of the circle.

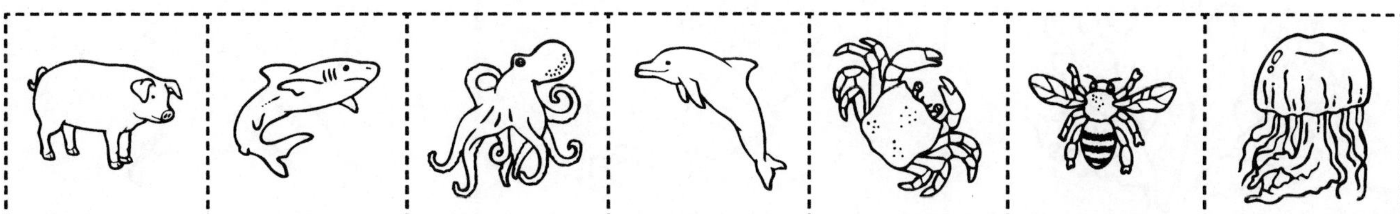

Warm-Up 30

The Creatures of the Coral Reefs

Name: ______________________________________

Coral reefs are made up of small animals covered in hard shells. These animals grow together. They form a community. A lot of animals live in and around this community.

Directions: Read about some types of coral and other animals who live in the reefs.

- Color the whole box **purple** if the animal is a type of coral.
- Color the whole box **blue** if the animal is a type of fish.
- Color the whole box **red** if the animal is not a fish or a type of coral.

Brain Coral This coral is shaped like the human brain. 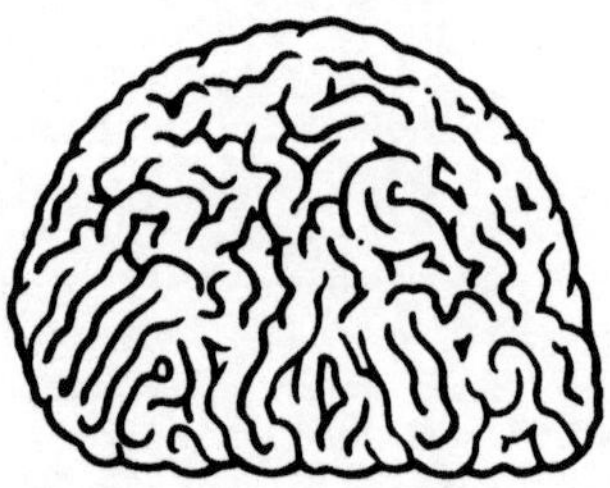	**Butterfly Fish** This fish has a large, eye-shaped spot. 	**Elkhorn Coral** This coral looks like an elk's antlers. 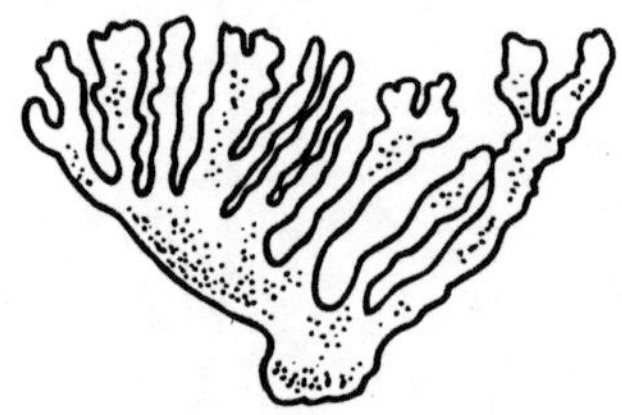
Lettuce Leaf Sea Slug This green sea slug has no shell. 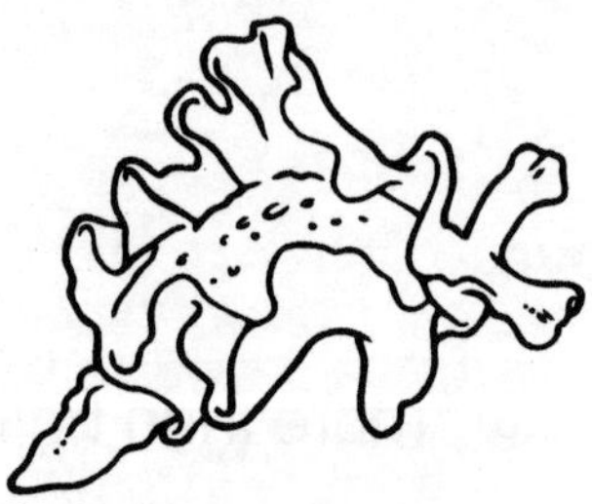	**Octopus** This animal has eight legs and can hide in the reef. 	**Queen Angelfish** This fish's flat body helps it fit in reefs. 
Seafans These coral move like small fans in the water. 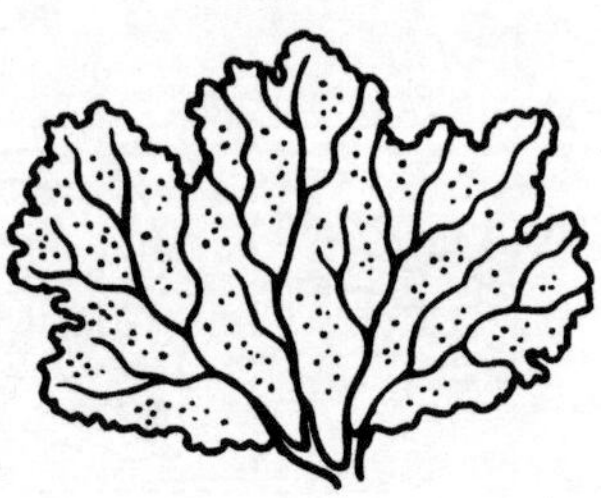	**Sea Horse** This unique fish looks like a tiny horse. 	**Sea Star** This is not a fish. It can regrow an arm if it loses one. 

Colorful Partners

Name: ______________________________

One colorful fish that lives among the coral reef is the clownfish. These fish have a lot of bright orange, black, and white colors. Some even have some red or yellow parts.

The sea anemone is also a colorful animal. It can be just about any color you can imagine. Anemones look like plants, but they are animals. They stick to a surface in the ocean and stay there.

Sea anemones can be very poisonous. That is how they get food. But they are also in danger of being harmed by certain creatures. They're stuck in one place, so how do they protect themselves from those creatures?

That's where the clownfish come in. Clownfish eat the creatures that harm the anemones. Also, clownfish are not harmed by the anemone's poison. Clownfish hide in the anemone so that they can't be eaten by bigger fish. The anemone and the clownfish protect each other. It works out well for both of them!

Directions: Look at the clownfish hiding by the anemone. Follow these rules:

- Color the **O** parts **ORANGE**.
- Color the **B** parts **BLACK**.
- Color the **P** parts **PURPLE**.
- Leave the other parts **WHITE**.

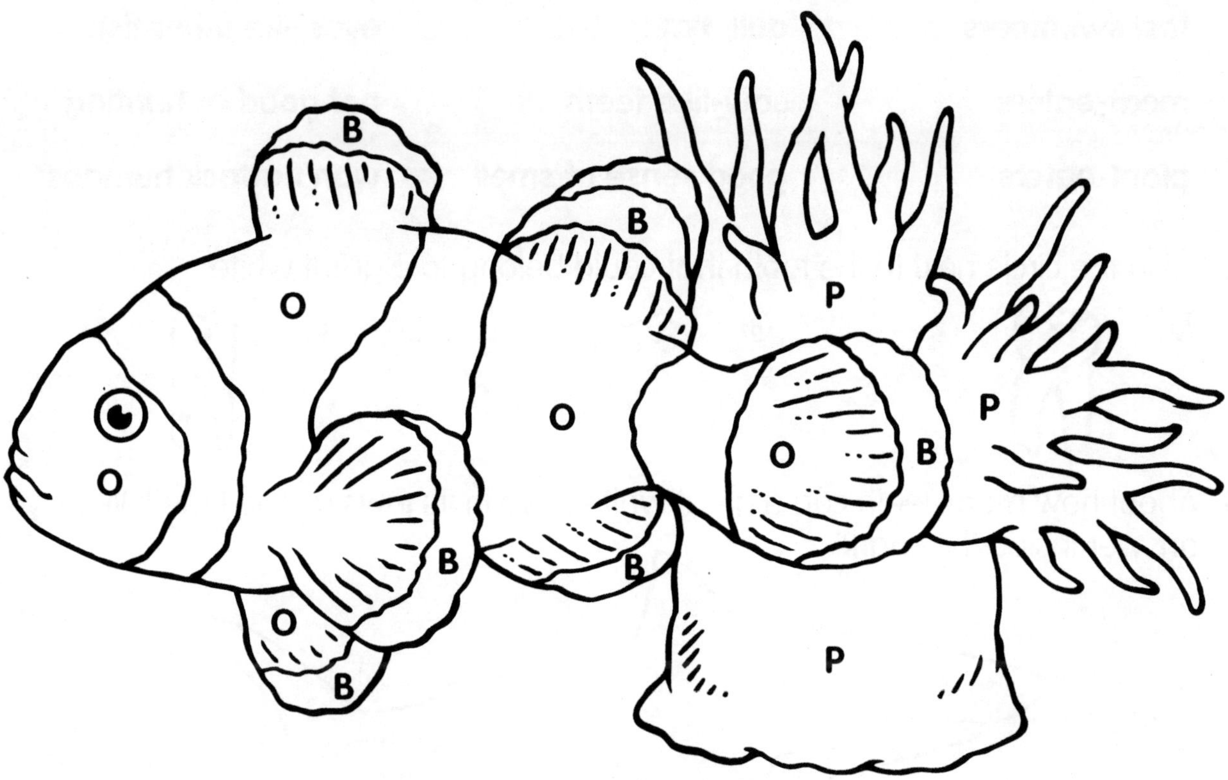

Warm-Up 32

One Feared Fish

Name: ______________________________

The great white shark may be the most feared creature in the ocean. So what makes these 2,000-pound animals so scary? Let's start with their teeth.

- A great white can have over 3,000 teeth in its mouth at one time. Each tooth is sharp and has saw-like edges. This type of tooth is perfect for tearing meat. Great whites can replace their lost teeth quickly.
- Great whites can smell a tiny drop of blood in lots of salt water. They can even tell where the smell is coming from.
- Their eyes can adapt to dark and light, just like a human's eyes do. The eyes of most fish cannot do this.
- Like other sharks, great whites can sense the electrical fields that other animals give off. This helps sharks find their prey (food).
- When attacking, great whites can swim over 25 miles per hour.
- Most sharks don't attack humans, but great white sharks sometimes do.

---

1. Cross out each word or group of words that **does not** describe great whites.

fast swimmers	**dull, flat teeth**	**eyes like other fish**
meat-eaters	**saw-like teeth**	**not good at hunting**
plant-eaters	**good sense of smell**	**won't attack humans**

2. Fill in the circle next to the tooth that could belong to a great white.

Ⓐ  Ⓑ  Ⓒ 

3. About how many teeth can a great white have in its jaws at one time? Write your answer inside the shark.

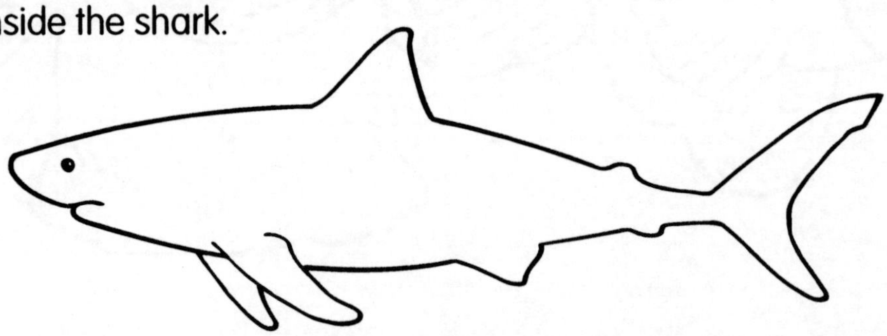

There's No Place Like Home

Name: ____________________________________

Not all water is the same. Most of Earth's water is salt water. The water in oceans and seas is salt water. Less than 3% of Earth's water is fresh water. This fresh water is found mostly in lakes and rivers. Most animals must live in either salt water or fresh water. They cannot survive in both.

One animal who can live in both fresh and salt water is the salmon. These fish are born in fresh water. Once they are strong enough, they travel far to live in the salty ocean. They live there for up to five years. When they are ready to reproduce (have babies), they make the long journey back to where they were born. Scientists have even been able to prove that salmon can return to the exact spot where they were born. It is thought that these fish use their sense of smell to do this. Once they are back in fresh water, they have their babies.

Directions: Look at the diagram below. This shows the journey a salmon takes. Each part of the journey is labeled. Point A shows where the journey begins, and Point C shows where it ends. Tell what kind of water each part of the journey takes place in. Write **salt** or **fresh** on the line below each point.

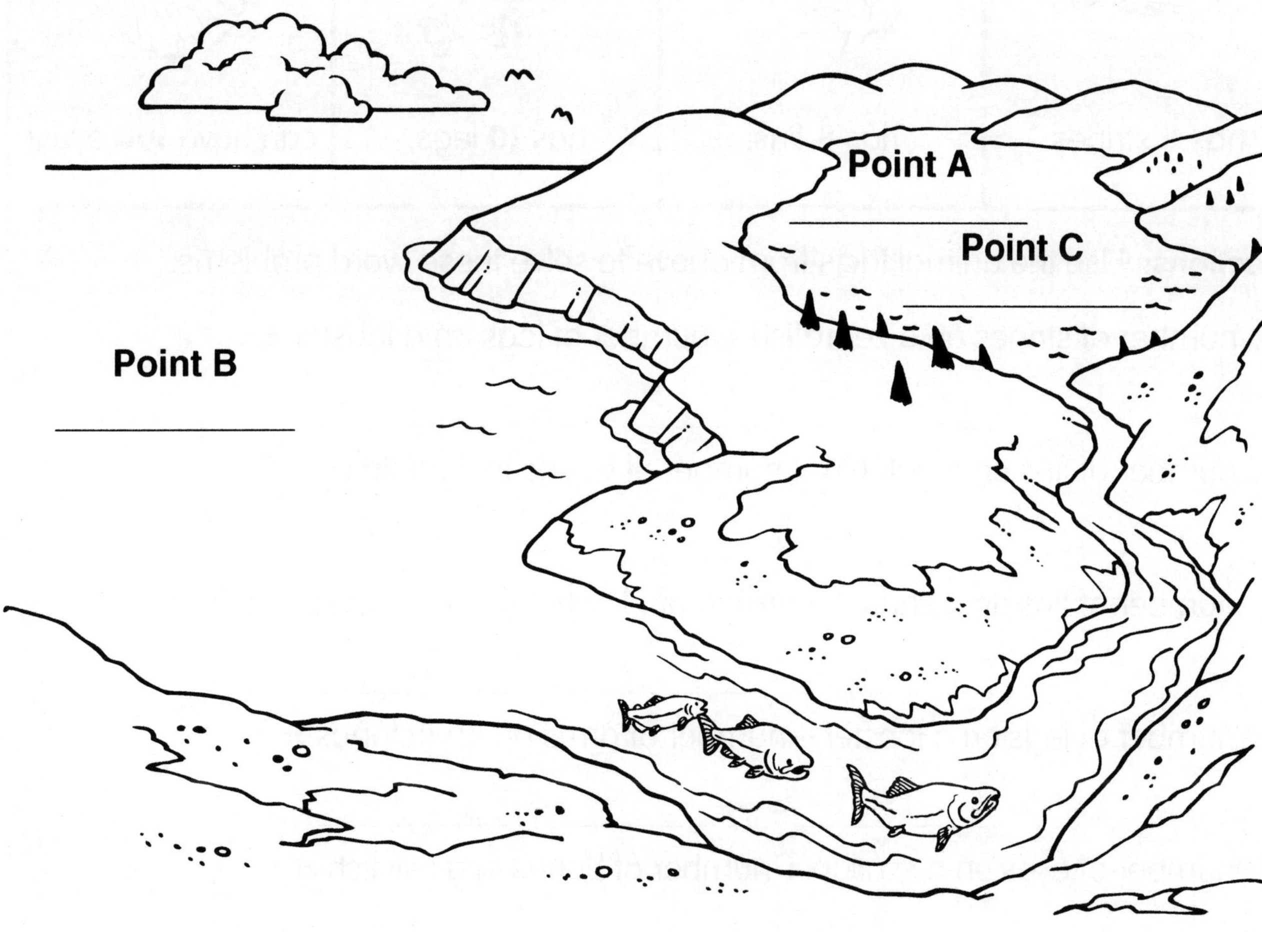

Warm-Up 34

Underwater-Animal Math

Name: ______________________________

You probably know that an octopus has 8 arms. But did you know about these other animal numbers?

A **jellyfish**	A **baleen whale**	A **squid**	A **dolphin**

has **0** bones.	has **2** blowholes.	has **3** hearts.	has **4** fins.
A **zebrafish**	A **shark**	A **lobster**	A **scallop**
		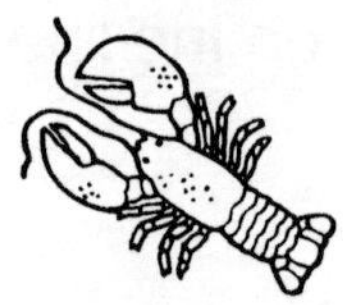	
has **5** stripes.	has **8** fins.	has **10** legs.	can have **100** eyes!

Directions: Use the animal facts from above to solve these word problems.

1. number of stripes on a zebrafish **+** number of legs on a lobster =

__________ + __________ = __________

2. number of fins on a dolphin **+** number of hearts in a squid =

__________ + __________ = __________

3. number of fins on a shark – number of blowholes on a baleen whale =

__________ – __________ = __________

4. number of legs on a lobster – number of arms on an octopus =

__________ – __________ = __________

5. number of eyes on a scallop **+** number of bones in a jellyfish =

__________ + __________ = __________

Have You Ever Seen a Sea Gorilla?

Name: ______________________________

You know that horses, cows, and lions are animals that live on land. But did you know that there are sea horses, sea cows, and sea lions? It's true!

Sea horses are small, bony fish. They swim upright and very slowly. They have curly tails and long snouts. Their heads look just like horse heads!

Manatees are big, thick mammals that are sometimes called **sea cows**. They weigh about 1,000 pounds. They have short flippers that look like paddles. They got their name because of the way they eat plants on the ocean floor. It reminds people of the way cows graze on grass.

Sea lions look a lot like seals. However, they are bigger and have different fur than seals. Some also have manes of hair around their faces, just like lions.

Directions: Can you imagine another ocean animal that is named after a land animal? It's time for you to create one. Describe it, draw a picture of it, and explain how it got its name.

Your Ocean Animal: ______________________________

Description: ______________________________

____

____

____

How It Got Its Name: ______________________________

____

____

____

Draw your animal here.

Warm-Up 36

Delicious, but Deadly

Name: ______________________________

The oceans and rivers are full of fish and other animals. People have counted on these animals for food for thousands of years.

One fish that people sometimes eat is the blowfish. In Japan, this fish is called *fugu*. Fugu is a very special fish. It is very expensive, and only certain chefs are allowed by law to serve it. Fugu is also the only food that the Emperor of Japan is not allowed to eat! What makes this fish so special?

Parts of fugu are very poisonous. These parts will kill anyone who eats them. The liver is one of the most poisonous parts. Since 1984, it has been illegal to serve fugu liver in a restaurant in Japan.

The chefs who prepare fugu must use a special knife to slice the safe parts of the fish away from the unsafe parts. This knife has a very thin blade. The poisoned parts cannot touch the safe parts or else they will make them unsafe.

Chefs must train for years before they are allowed to serve fugu. They must take many tests. Fewer than half of the chefs are able to pass all of the tests. At the end of training, each chef has to prepare and eat fugu. Some chefs die while taking this test!

After reading all of this, can you believe that fugu is a very popular dish in Japan? It is! Some people say that it is incredibly delicious. They say it is worth every penny and also worth the danger. Some even demand to be served the liver. They are proud when they eat fugu liver and live to tell the tale.

Directions: Choose just one of these story starters. Write it on a separate piece of paper. Then, finish your story. Write at least three sentences.

1. I was at a restaurant in Japan. A friend ordered a plate of fugu for me.

2. I am starting my training tomorrow. I am studying to be a fugu chef!

3. I am a great fugu chef. A famous customer has just demanded that I serve him fugu liver.

Name: ______________________________

What do you do if you read a word that you have never seen before? If you don't have a dictionary or computer nearby, how can you know the meaning of the word?

Sometimes you can guess a word's meaning by how it is used. In this way, you can figure out what it means, even if you have never seen or heard it before.

Directions: Read each statement about an animal that lives in the water. Each sentence includes a **boldfaced** word. Use the clues to guess the meaning of that word. Fill in the circle next to the correct answer.

1. Blue whales are **colossal**. They can grow to almost 100 feet in length. That makes them the largest animals on Earth.

   From this statement, you can guess that the word **colossal** most likely means

   Ⓐ fast. Ⓑ slow. Ⓒ big. Ⓓ hungry.

2. Dolphins are **social** animals. Groups of dolphins are called *pods*. Sometimes, dolphins even form *superpods*, which are made up of about 1,000 dolphins.

   From this statement, you can guess that the word **social** tells you that dolphins

   Ⓐ are as smart as humans.
   Ⓑ often live together.
   Ⓒ cannot breathe underwater.
   Ⓓ do not eat meat.

3. Great white sharks are **predatory** animals. These meat-eating sharks search for animals swimming near the surface of the water. The great whites then quickly swim up under the animals and attack them.

   From this statement, you can guess that a **predatory** animal

   Ⓐ leaves other animals alone.
   Ⓑ warns animals to stay away.
   Ⓒ hides from other animals.
   Ⓓ hunts and kills other animals.

4. It is **treacherous** to bother a blue-ringed octopus. They will bite people who poke them or step on them. This octopus is one of the ocean's most poisonous creatures. Its venom can kill people.

   From this statement, you can guess that the word **treacherous** most likely means

   Ⓐ dangerous and unsafe.
   Ⓑ difficult and impossible.
   Ⓒ strange and unusual.
   Ⓓ fun and interesting.

Warm-Up 38

This Land Is Our Land... and Theirs, Too

Name: ______________________________

We live on land. We cannot survive underwater like fish can. There are a lot of animals that are like us in this way. These animals live on land, too.

Some animals that live on land are very big, like elephants. Others are very small, like insects and spiders. These animals are different in many ways, but they all must live on land. Why? One big reason is that they all need to breathe air.

We live very close to lots of animals. Think about insects and spiders. These tiny animals are everywhere. Some are pests, but others help flowers grow. Now think about farm animals, like cows and chickens. They provide us with milk and eggs and food. There are even animals that live with us in our homes. They are our pets.

What Did You Learn ?

1. What is one way that elephants, insects, and people are alike?

Ⓐ They all need air to breathe.

Ⓑ They all walk on two legs.

Ⓒ They all are good swimmers.

2. Choose the words that would best complete this sentence:

We ______________________ other animals.

Ⓐ do not live near

Ⓑ have nothing in common with

Ⓒ share the land with

3. Land animals come in all sizes. Put these animals in order from smallest to biggest. Put a **1** next to the smallest animal. Put a **6** next to the biggest.

________ **cat**

________ **elephant**

________ **horse**

________ **mouse**

________ **person**

________ **spider**

Getting Around on Land

Warm-Up 39

Name: ______________________________

There are many ways to get around on land. We walk around on two feet. Can you think of any other animals that do that?

Directions: Each word below describes a way to get around on land. Think about the animals you have seen before or have read about. How do they get around? Under each word, write the name of at least one animal that gets around that way. The first one has been done for you. (**Hint:** Remember, insects and reptiles are animals, too.)

Walks on Two Feet	**Walks on Four Feet**
human ______________	______________ ______________
Crawls	**Jumps**
______________ ______________	______________ ______________
Hops	**Swings**
______________ ______________	______________ ______________

Can you think of any other ways of getting around? Write two more ways. Under each, write the name of an animal that gets around that way.

______________	______________
______________ ______________	______________ ______________

Warm-Up 40

Mammals and More

Name: ______________________________

All kinds of animals walk, crawl, and hop around on land. Four of the most common types of land animals are mammals, reptiles, amphibians, and invertebrates.

- **Mammals** — These animals are warm-blooded. Most give birth to live young.
  Examples: humans, apes, dogs, cats, cows, horses, pigs, mice, elephants
- **Reptiles** — These animals are cold-blooded. They have scales. They lay eggs. Their young hatch from these eggs.
  Examples: snakes, lizards, crocodiles, turtles
- **Amphibians** — These animals are cold-blooded. They often start out living in water and then move to land.
  Examples: frogs, newts, salamanders
- **Invertebrates** — These animals are cold-blooded. They do not have a backbone.
  Examples: insects, spiders, worms, snails

Directions: Look at the name of each animal below.

- If the animal is a **mammal**, color the space **brown**.
- If the animal is a **reptile**, color the space **green**.
- If the animal is an **amphibian**, color the space **yellow**.
- If the animal is an **invertebrate**, color the space **orange**.

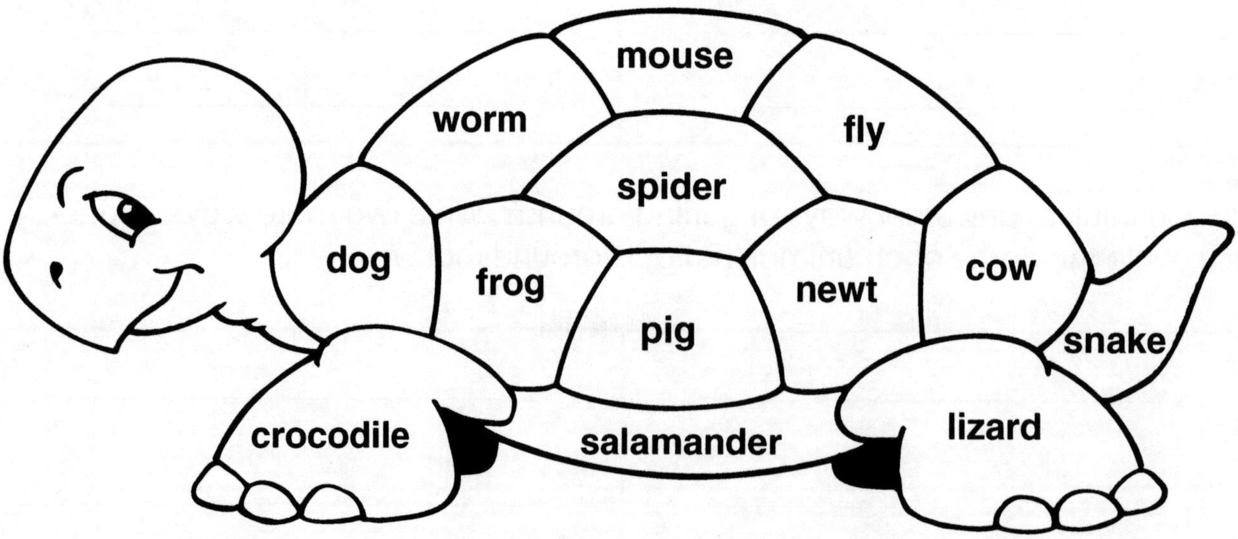

Look at the big picture. What kind of animal do you see? (Circle one.)

mammal **reptile** **amphibian** **invertebrate**

All Kinds of Coverings

Warm-Up 41

Name: ____________________________________

There are so many different types of animals that walk around on land. Some look similar to each other, while others look completely different. Some have feathers, some have fur, some have scales, and some have shells.

Directions: Look at the list of land animals. Use what you already know to match each animal to the kind of covering it has. Write the name of the animal in the correct category below.

lion	lizard	ostrich	peacock	polar bear

snail	**snake**	**turkey**	**turtle**	**wolf**

Feathers	Fur	Scales	Shells
1. ____________	1. ____________	1. ____________	1. ____________
2. ____________	2. ____________	2. ____________	2. ____________
3. ____________	3. ____________		

Warm-Up 42

Which Land Animal Is Which?

Name: ____

Some animals are very much like other animals. You may even hear one called the same name as the other. But they are not exactly alike.

Directions: Look at each pair of animals. Use the clue to name the animal that is pictured. Write the animal's name on the line.

1. Frog vs. Toad

Frogs need to live near water. Toads do not.

Which animal is this?

____

2. Snail vs. Slug

Snails have a shell. Slugs do not.

Which animal is this?

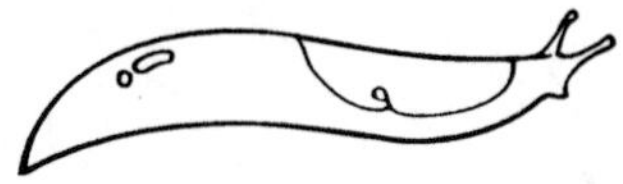

____

3. Alligator vs. Crocodile

Crocodiles have a tooth sticking out of their mouth. This tooth is covered in an alligator's mouth.

Which animal is this?

____

4. Turtle vs. Tortoise

Turtles need to live near water. Tortoises do not.

Which animal is on the **left**?

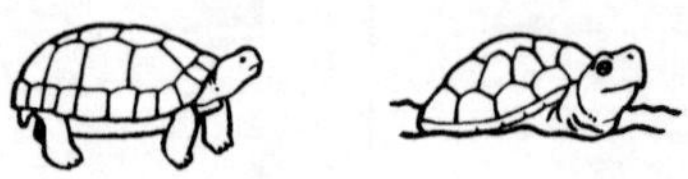

____

5. Rat vs. Mouse

A rat is much bigger than a mouse. Which animal is on **top** of the box?

____

Trace the Snakes . . . If You Dare!

Name: ____________________________________

A lot of people are afraid of snakes. They slither and hiss, and some are deadly!

Directions: Color along each path to find the fact that matches each dangerous snake. Use a different color for each snake. Write the snake number below each tail.

- Use **red** for Snake 1.
- Use **green** for Snake 2.
- Use **black** for Snake 3.
- Use **orange** for Snake 4.

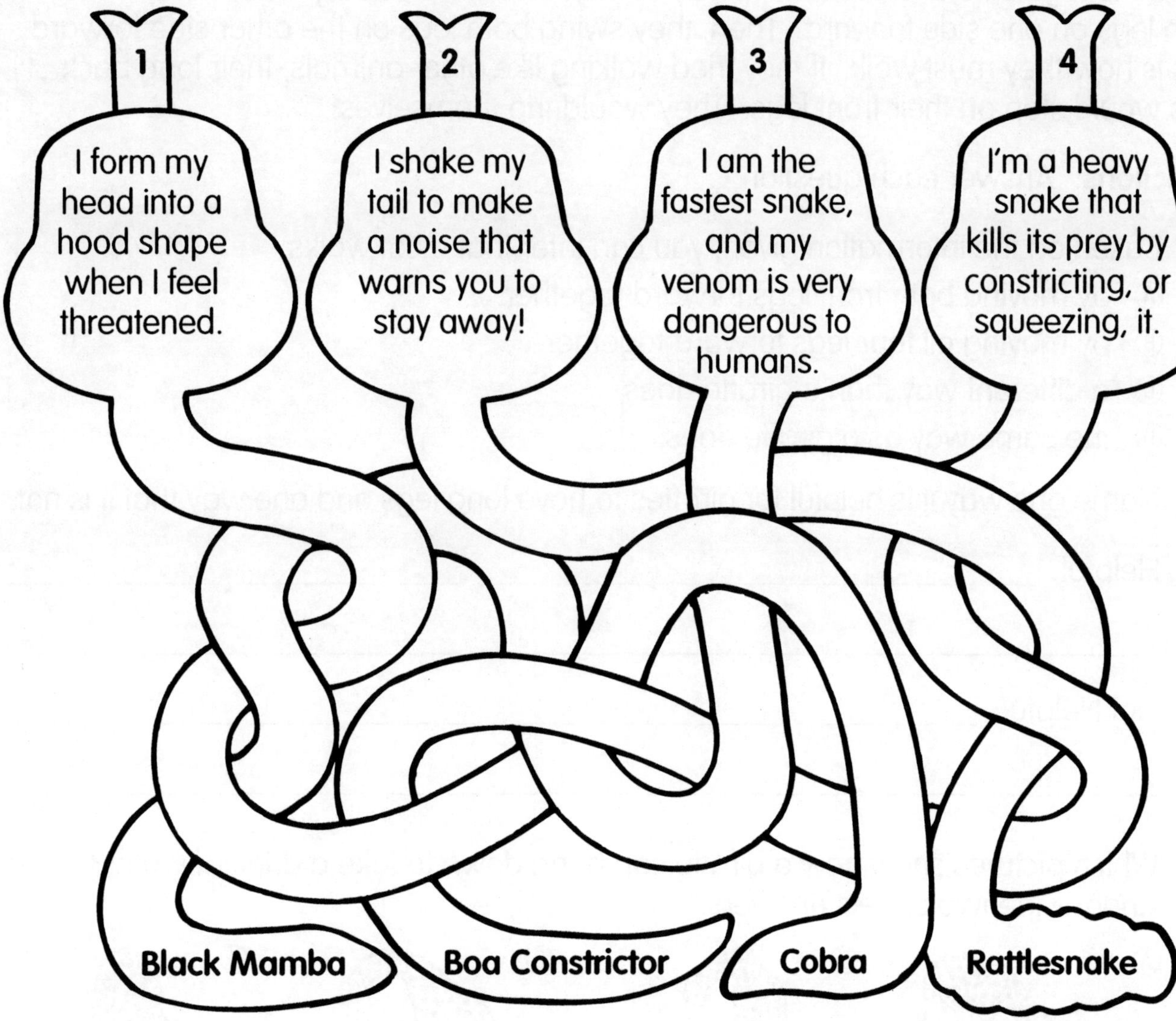

Snake # _____ Snake # _____ Snake # _____ Snake # _____

Warm-Up 44

The Trouble with Long Legs

Name: ______________________________

Giraffes are the tallest animals on land. They also have the longest legs. They can use these legs to protect themselves. Mother giraffes will kick at animals that are attacking their babies. But these long legs cause problems for giraffes, too.

Giraffes need to drink water. They must get low to the ground to do this. Their long legs can make this difficult. Giraffes either must spread their front legs wide open or they must bend their knees. They cannot just drop their heads down to the ground without doing one of these things.

Giraffes must also walk differently than other four-footed animals. Giraffes have to move the legs on one side of their body at the same time as they walk. They swing both legs on one side forward. Then, they swing both legs on the other side forward. This is how they must walk. If they tried walking like other animals, their long back legs would step on their front legs. They would trip themselves!

Directions: Answer each question.

1. Based on the information given, you can infer that a cat walks

Ⓐ by moving both front legs forward together.

Ⓑ by moving all four legs forward together.

Ⓒ a different way than a giraffe does.

Ⓓ the same way as a giraffe does.

2. Name one way it is helpful for giraffes to have long legs and one way that it is not.

Helpful: ______________________________

____

Not Helpful: ______________________________

____

3. Which pictures show how a giraffe can bend down to take a drink of water? Choose the two correct answers.

Ⓐ

Ⓑ

Ⓒ

Ⓓ

Warm-Up 45

Name: ______________________________

If you look closely at the names of some animals, you can find other words.

Directions: Use a small word from the box to complete the name of each land animal below.

ant	ear	or
arm	key	pan
bit	nail	pen
cup	on	use

1. l i ___ ___

2. w ___ ___ m
3. b ___ ___ ___
4. r a b ___ ___ ___
5. s ___ ___ ___ ___

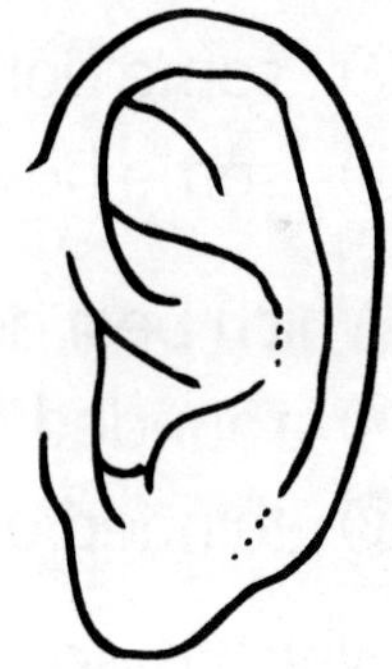

6. e l e p h ___ ___ ___
7. ___ ___ ___ g u i n
8. m o ___ ___ ___

9. m o n ___ ___ ___
10. ___ ___ ___ d a
11. ___ ___ ___ a d i l l o
12. p o r ___ ___ ___ i n e

Warm-Up 46

How Do They Get Up There?

Name: ______________________________

Have you ever dreamed of flying in the sky? Many people have. They see birds fly, and it looks like it would be fun. Birds also make flying look easy. However, there are many reasons why birds can fly and we can't.

Most birds do not weigh much. This is very important. Birds that weigh over 30 pounds (like ostriches) cannot get up off the ground. Birds also have very powerful chest muscles. A bird's chest muscles make up about 15% of its entire weight. These muscles help birds flap their wings up and down.

Birds' wings are the main reason that most can fly. Birds use their wings to press air down. This motion lifts them up. The shape of a bird's wings also helps it to move forward as it lifts up. Its wings are curved. They are rounded at the front, and they thin out toward the back of the wing.

People have studied the shape of birds' wings. We have studied the way birds push air down. We have used this information to build airplanes. We have used this knowledge to build machines that can help us fly through the sky.

What Did You Learn?

1. Some birds can't fly. What is one reason the story gives for this fact?

Ⓐ some don't have wings
Ⓑ some have small chest muscles
Ⓒ some don't know how
Ⓓ some are too heavy

2. Which best describes a bird's wings?

Ⓐ rounded at the front, thinned out toward the back
Ⓑ thinned out at the front, rounded toward the back

3. Which machine most flies like a bird?

Ⓐ 

Ⓑ 

Ⓒ 

Now look at the picture of the bird. Draw an arrow to show which direction its wings push air as it flies.

Taking Turns at the Front

Name: ______________________________

Birds often fly in groups. The group forms the shape of the letter V. Groups can fly in this V-shape for a long time. Why do they do this?

Imagine a bird flying into wind. The wind pushes back at the bird. This makes it harder to fly. The bird must use a lot of energy. When birds fly together, they use less energy. This is because the bird in front flies into the most wind. The birds behind the front bird meet a little less wind. The front bird blocks it from them. This happens all the way through the group, so the birds in the back don't meet up with much wind at all. The air at the back of the group is easier to fly through.

This makes flying hard on the bird in front. When that bird gets tired, it drops to the back where flying is easier. Another bird takes its turn flying in front. In this way, all of the birds get a chance to rest as they fly.

Directions: Look at the picture. It shows a group of five birds flying in the V-shape.

- Draw a **blue circle** around the two birds that are meeting the least amount of wind.
- Draw a **red square** around the bird that is working the hardest.
- What if this group had 7 birds in it? Draw **2 more** birds to show where they would fly as part of the V-shape.

Warm-Up 48

Some Birds Cannot Fly

Name: ______________________________________

Most birds can fly through the air. Some birds, however, cannot fly. These birds are called flightless birds. Flightless birds have smaller wing bones than birds that can fly. Flightless birds also have more feathers than other birds. Penguins, ostriches, and emus are flightless birds.

Penguins have very short wings. These wings are more like flippers. They help penguins to be great swimmers.

Ostriches are the heaviest birds. They have powerful legs. Ostriches can run faster than any other bird.

Emus are large birds from Australia. Their feathers don't let heat in. This allows emus to walk around under the hot, afternoon sun.

Directions: Read each statement. Write **true** or **false** on the line to the left. If the statement is false, underline the word(s) that make it false. Write the word(s) that would make it true on the line to the right. The first one has been done for you.

__false__ **1.** Penguins and emus are <u>flying</u> birds. __flightless__

________ **2.** A penguin's wings are more like flippers. ________

________ **3.** A penguin's wings make it a great flier. ________

________ **4.** Ostriches are the heaviest birds. ________

________ **5.** Ostriches run faster than any other animal. ________

________ **6.** Emus are large birds from Africa. ________

________ **7.** Emus can walk around on very hot days. ________

________ **8.** Flightless birds have fewer feathers than other birds. ________

Surprise, These Creatures Can Fly!

Name: ______________________________________

When we look up in the sky, we expect to see birds and insects flying. But would you ever expect to see one of these animals in the air?

Flying Fish

These creatures have very long fins that they can use like wings. They leap out of the water and then use their fins to glide through the air. They can "fly" as far as 650 feet!

Flying Lizards

These small creatures live in forests. They use folds of skin to help them glide from tree to tree. They can glide over 30 feet.

Flying Snakes

These snakes live high up in forests. They flatten their bodies as they jump off trees. They glide through the air, twisting and reshaping their bodies. This helps them glide for up to 330 feet!

Flying Squirrels

These mammals have skin that stretches from their ankles to their wrists. This skin forms a parachute when they jump out of trees. This helps them glide about 150 feet from tree to tree.

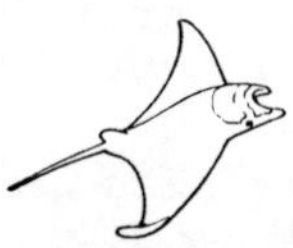

Mobula Rays

These large, heavy creatures can fling themselves out of the ocean. Some can glide as high as 7 feet above the water. Watch out, they sometimes land on boats that are passing by!

Directions: Answer these questions. Explain your answers.

1. These animals are in order by how far they can "fly." Write in the missing names and distances.

Animal	Lizard	Squirrel		Fish
Distance	30 feet		330 feet	

2. Which one of these animals would you most like to see "fly"? Why? ____________

____

____

Warm-Up 50

Riders on the Wind

Name: ______________________________

There is a bird that can fly for months at a time. It can fly millions of miles in its lifetime. This bird can fly as fast as a car on a highway, and it can also sleep while it's flying. It can do all of this without flapping its wings very much. This bird is called an albatross, and it really knows how to ride the wind.

Albatrosses fly over the ocean. They use the wind to glide and soar. They use the wind to swoop down to the water to get their food. How is the albatross so good at using the wind? It all has to do with this bird's wings.

Albatrosses have very long wings. A bird's wingspan is the measurement from the tip of one wing to the tip of the other. An albatross's wingspan can be almost 12 feet across. That is about two times the length of an adult man! The albatross's wings are also very narrow. Such long, narrow wings make the albatross the greatest glider in the animal world.

Part 1 Directions: Fill in the circle next to each correct answer.

1. Which pair of words best describes an albatross in flight?

Ⓐ flapping and rising
Ⓑ soaring and gliding
Ⓒ fluttering and dipping
Ⓓ hovering and darting

2. Which pair of words best describes an albatross's wings?

Ⓐ short and thick
Ⓑ long and thick
Ⓒ short and narrow
Ⓓ long and narrow

3. Most likely, an albatross mainly eats

Ⓐ animals that fly.
Ⓑ animals that live on land.
Ⓒ animals that live near the water surface.

Part 2 Directions: Unscramble the cloud of letters to make a word that means "the measurement from the tip of one wing to the tip of the other." Cross out each letter as you use it. A few letters have been placed for you.

w ___ ___ ___ s ___ ___ n

The Teeny-Tiny, Backwards-Flying Bird

Warm-Up 51

Name: ______________________________

Can you imagine a bird that weighs less than a penny? That is how tiny and light a hummingbird can be. Hummingbirds are small in size, but that doesn't mean they are not interesting.

Hummingbirds fly around looking for nectar to eat. They get this nectar from flowers. They will only drink nectar that has a lot of sugar in it. It must be sweet. When they find a flower, they hover over the flower as they drink. They hover in mid-air like a helicopter does. How do they do this? They flap their wings really fast. Hummingbirds can flap their wings up to 80 times per second. That's too fast to even see! Flapping their wings that fast takes a lot of energy. Hummingbirds cannot fly all day. In fact, they must rest for about 16 hours each day.

Directions: Fill in the circle next to each correct answer.

1. Which of these is something that the story says a hummingbird cannot do?

Ⓐ fly backwards
Ⓑ hover in mid-air
Ⓒ flap their wings fast
Ⓓ spend all day flying

2. The smallest hummingbirds weigh ____________ a penny.

Ⓐ the same as
Ⓑ less than
Ⓒ more than

3. If a person had the same taste in food as a hummingbird, which of these foods would he or she most likely want to eat?

Ⓐ 

Ⓑ 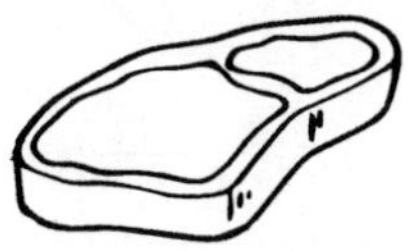

Ⓒ 

Ⓓ 

4. The graph below shows the number of hours in a day. Each block equals two hours. Use your pencil to shade in all of the hours that a hummingbird rests each day.

2	4	6	8	10	12	14	16	18	20	22	24

Warm-Up 52

Birds of a Feather...

Name: ______________________________

There is an old saying that goes, "Birds of a feather flock together." It means that people who are alike often hang out together. This saying makes sense because birds often fly in groups. They stick together. This helps keep them safe.

A group of birds together is called a *flock*. There are different names, though, for groups of each type of bird.

Directions: Look at the names in the box. They are the names of different groups of birds. Some of the names are very odd! Use the clues and the letters given to figure out the names of each group of birds.

Names Box

band	kettle	pod
flight	murder	raft

1. Clues
name for a group of pelicans;
sounds like what peas come in

___ o ___

2. Clues
name for a group of doves;
sounds like a trip on a plane

___ l ___ ___ ___ t

3. Clues
name for a group of jays;
sounds like they play instruments

___ a ___ ___

4. Clues
name for a group of ducks;
sounds like something you float on

___ ___ ___ ___

5. Clues
name for a group of hawks;
sounds like what you make tea in

___ ___ ___ ___ ___ ___

6. Clues
name for a group of crows;
sounds like a terrible crime

___ ___ ___ ___ ___ ___

Which group name do you think is most interesting? ______________________

Why? ______________________________

Warm-Up 53

Name: ______________________________

Let's say someone described a bird they saw in the sky. What if they said that it was flying? Would that tell you much about what the bird was doing?

The word *flying* is very basic. It doesn't tell you *how* something is flying. There are words that can do that much better.

Directions: Read each sentence. What word would best describe how the animal is flying? Use the words in the **Word Box** to help you. Some letters have also been filled in for each answer.

Word Box

flapping	gliding	soaring
fluttering	hovering	swooping

1. The eagle was going higher and higher up into the sky.

The eagle was s ___ ___ r ___ n ___.

2. The butterfly was lightly bouncing from plant to plant.

The butterfly was ___ l ___ ___ t ___ ___ i ___ ___.

3. The hummingbird was hanging in mid-air above the flower.

The hummingbird was ___ o ___ e ___ i ___ ___.

4. The pelican quickly dove down to pluck a fish from the sea.

The pelican was s ___ ___ o ___ ___ ___ ___.

5. The pigeon was beating its wings up and down as it flew.

The pigeon was ___ ___ a ___ ___ ___ n ___.

6. The falcon stretched its wings out and let the wind move it along.

The falcon was ___ ___ i d ___ ___ ___.

Warm-Up 54

They Come in All Shapes and Sizes

Name: ______________________________

Animals come in all sizes. Some can fit in your lap. Others can fit on the tip of your fingernail. Some are bigger than your bedroom.

The blue whale is one animal that is huge. This gentle mammal lives in the ocean. It can grow to be almost 100 feet long. That is longer than the distance from home plate to first base on a pro baseball field.

Not everything in the ocean is big. There is one type of jellyfish that is about half the size of a dime. This jellyfish is tiny, but it is also dangerous. Its sting is painful.

Animals come in different colors, too. Can you believe that there are blue lobsters, pink dolphins, and orange frogs? There is even a snail with a purple shell! It lives in warm, shallow ocean water.

What Did You Learn ?

1. Which kind of animal is **not** talked about in the story?
   - Ⓐ pink dolphin
   - Ⓑ yellow frog
   - Ⓒ blue lobster
   - Ⓓ blue whale

2. What type of animal is a whale?
   - Ⓐ a fish
   - Ⓑ an insect
   - Ⓒ a mammal
   - Ⓓ a reptile

3. Which animal mentioned in the story is most likely bigger than your bedroom?
   - Ⓐ blue lobster
   - Ⓑ pink dolphin
   - Ⓒ purple snail
   - Ⓓ blue whale

4. Draw lines to match each animal to the word that best describes it.

jellyfish	**gentle**
blue lobster	**dangerous**
blue whale	**unusual**

The Long, Slow Life of a Tortoise

Warm-Up 55

Name: ______________________________

Some animals live a very long time. Others do not. This graph shows how long some animals can live.

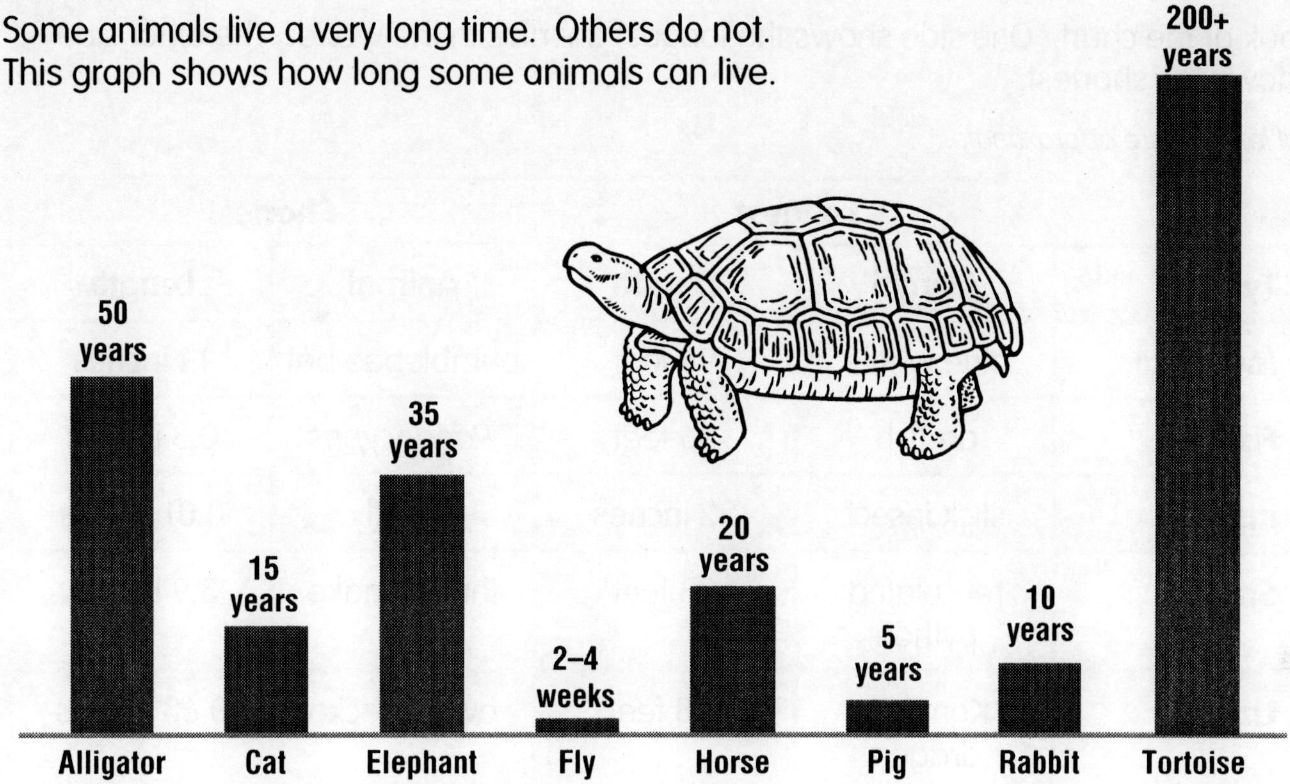

Part 1 Directions: Read each statement. If it is true, write a **T** on the line. If it is false, write an **F**. Use the graph to help you.

_________ **1.** Elephants can live for 100 years.

_________ **2.** A rabbit can live for about 10 years.

_________ **3.** Flies can't even live for one year.

_________ **4.** No animal can live as long as a cat can.

Part 2 Directions: Put these animals in age order from longest to shortest. Write **1st** in the box above the one that lives the longest. Write **2nd** in the box above the one that lives the second longest. Write **3rd** in the box above the one that lives the shortest amount of time.

horse	**fly**	**pig**

Warm-Up 56

The Long and the Short of It

Name: ______________________________

Look at the chart. One side shows the longest animals in the world. The other side shows the shortest.

All lengths are approximate.

	Longest		Shortest	
Type	**Animal**	**Length**	**Animal**	**Length**
Mammal	blue whale	98 feet	bumblebee bat	1.1 inches
Fish	oarfish	56 feet	*Paedocypris*	0.3 inches
Insect	stick insect	22 inches	fairy fly	0.01 inches
Snake	reticulated python	33 feet	threadsnake	3.9 inches
Lizard	Komodo dragon	9.8 feet	dwarf gecko	0.63 inches

Directions: Use the chart to answer each question. Circle each correct answer.

1. Which is longer? **the longest fish** **the longest snake**

2. Which is shorter? **the shortest lizard** **the shortest mammal**

3. Which is shorter? **the longest lizard** **the longest fish**

What Am I ?

I may be thin, but I'm very long. My body can be up to 14 inches long. With my legs stretched out, I'm even longer. What do I look like? My name says it all!

I am a ____ ____ ____ ____ ____ **insect.**

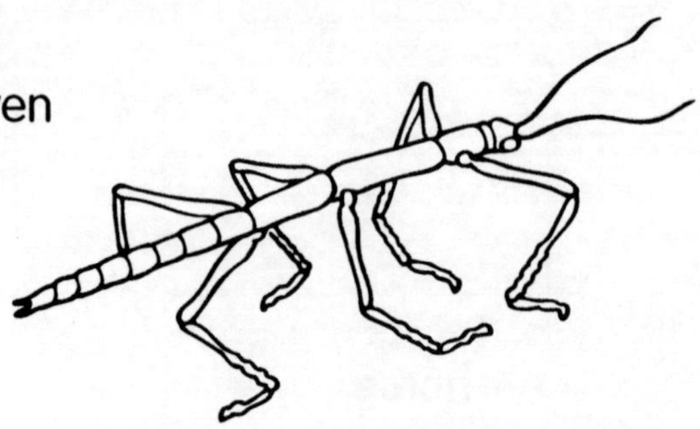

Never Challenge a Cheetah to a Race

Name: ______________________________

No land animal is faster than the cheetah. It can run up to 70 miles per hour. That's as fast as a car speeding on the freeway! How can a cheetah run so much faster than other animals? It's all about how a cheetah is built.

Directions: Look at the picture of the cheetah. The names of her body parts are all scrambled up! Unscramble the letters to name the parts that allow her to run so fast.

Hint: The first letter in each word is **darker** than the others.

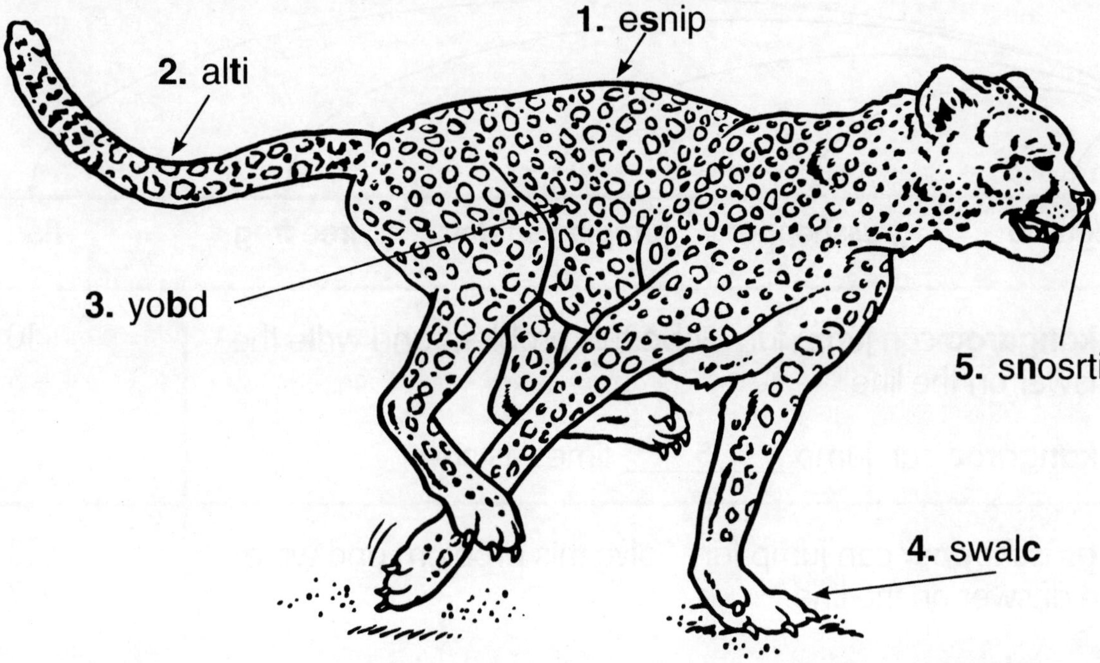

1. The cheetah's ____ ____ ____ ____ ____ is very flexible. It can bend a lot as she runs.

2. The cheetah's ____ ____ ____ ____ is long and flat. This helps her turn suddenly at high speeds.

3. The cheetah's ____ ____ ____ ____ is light and lean. Her low weight helps her gain speed quickly.

4. The cheetah's ____ ____ ____ ____ ____ always stick out. They give her a great grip on the ground as she runs.

5. Her ____ ____ ____ ____ ____ ____ ____ ____ are large and wide. This helps her breathe in a lot of oxygen as she runs.

Warm-Up 58

Nature's Best Jumpers

Name: ______________________________

How far can you jump? The best jump ever recorded by a person is 30 feet. That is about five times that person's size! Most people can't jump anywhere near that far. Some animals, however, can jump much farther.

Directions: Look at the number line. It shows how far each animal can jump in relation to its size. Do the math problems below to find out how far each animal can jump. The first one is done for you.

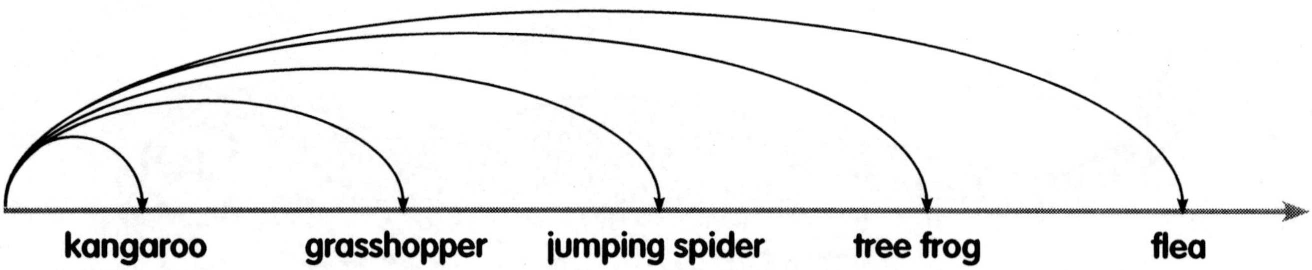

1. A **kangaroo** can jump far. Solve this problem and write the answer on the line. A **kangaroo** can jump ___5___ times its size.	10 – 5 **5**
2. A **grasshopper** can jump far. Solve this problem and write the answer on the line. A **grasshopper** can jump ________ times its size.	13 + 7
3. A **jumping spider** can jump far. Solve this problem and write the answer on the line. A **jumping spider** can jump ________ times its size.	81 + 19
4. A **tree frog** can jump far. Solve this problem and write the answer on the line. A **tree frog** can jump ________ times its size.	165 – 15
5. A **flea** can jump *really* far. Solve this problem and write the answer on the line. A **flea** can jump ________ times its size.	150 + 70

Warm-Up 59

Name: ______________________________

Directions: Look at the clues. Think about what you already know about each animal. Put it all together to answer each question.

Clues Box

- A giraffe needs to pump blood from its heart to its brain.
- Giraffes have the highest blood pressure of any animal. Their hearts have to work harder than any other animal to pump their blood.

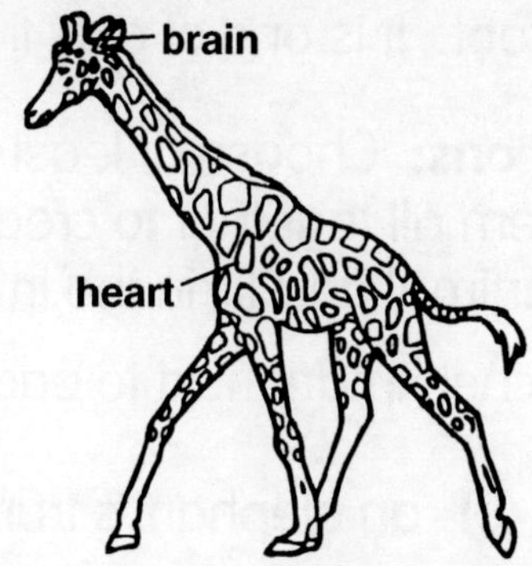

1. Why do you think a giraffe's heart would have to pump its blood at a higher pressure than other animals?

____

____

____

Clues Box

- Some birds of prey fly as high as 10,000 feet above the ground.
- These birds often swoop down to grab and eat small rodents that crawl on the ground.
- Birds of prey can see about four times better than humans.

2. What is one reason a bird of prey would need to have great eyesight in order to survive?

____

____

____

Warm-Up 60

Can You Make a More Extreme Animal?

Name: ______________________________

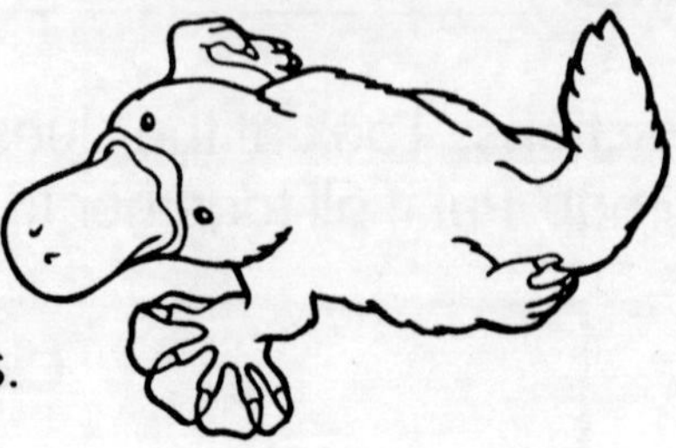

Is there any animal more odd than the platypus? It has the bill of a duck, the tail of a beaver, and the feet of an otter. It can inject poison from its back foot. It is one of only five mammals that can lay eggs.

Directions: Choose at least four of the most extreme parts from different animals. Put them all together to create a new animal that is as strange as a platypus. Draw your animal and fill in the information about it.

Put a checkmark next to each animal part you choose:

- ❑ an elephant's trunk
- ❑ a giraffe's neck
- ❑ a kangaroo's pouch
- ❑ a lion's mane
- ❑ an owl's eyes
- ❑ a peacock's feathers
- ❑ a porcupine's spikes
- ❑ a ram's horns
- ❑ a rattlesnake's tail
- ❑ a shark's teeth
- ❑ a turtle's shell
- ❑ a zebra's stripes

Draw Your Animal Here:

Name of Animal: ______________________________

What It Eats: ______________________________

One Amazing "Fact" About the Animal: ______________________________

____

Warm-Up 61

Name: ________________________________

Part 1 Directions: For each sentence, look at the underlined vocabulary word. Fill in the circle next to the answer that tells how the word is used in the sentence.

1. An elephant has a larger **trunk** than any other animal in the world.
   - Ⓐ a large suitcase
   - Ⓑ a place for storage in a car
   - Ⓒ a body part that is like a nose

2. Unlike those of other animals, a rhinoceros's large **horn** does not contain any bone.
   - Ⓐ a part of a car used to warn other drivers
   - Ⓑ a hard growth on the head of an animal
   - Ⓒ a musical instrument

Part 2 Directions: Choose a word from the box that best completes each idea and write the word on the line.

cent	**clause**	**hair**	**heir**	**scent**	**tooths**
Claus	**claws**	**hare**	**sent**	**teeth**	**toothes**

3. Skunks use an awful-smelling ______________________ to chase away enemies. The odor is so bad, people can smell it from a mile away.

4. Sharks are known for their sharp, scary-looking ______________________. Did you know that sharks can lose and grow over 30,000 of them during their lifetime?

5. Cheetahs have special ______________________ that help them run faster. They are great for gripping the ground.

6. The ______________________ on a sloth's body grows in the opposite direction than it does on other animals. This is because sloths spend a lot of their time hanging upside-down.

Warm-Up 62

The Problems Animals Can Face

Name: ____________________________________

Sometimes a type of animal becomes *endangered*. That means that type of animal is in danger of dying out. There will be no more left in the world if that happens. When there are no more left of a type of animal, that animal is *extinct*. Think of dinosaurs. There are no more dinosaurs. They are extinct.

Why do some animals become endangered or extinct? There are many reasons. People are often the cause. People use the land where animals live. This makes food and safe shelter harder to find. People also cause *pollution*.

Pollution is when dangerous chemicals get into the air, soil, or water. These chemicals make animals sick. People also move animals into new places. This can change the environment. The new animals may eat all of the animals that already lived there.

Sometimes animals become endangered or extinct because they don't have enough babies. Sometimes they have too many enemies and no way of protecting themselves. There are many reasons why animals can become endangered or extinct.

What Did You Learn ?

1. A dodo was a type of bird that died out completely. Dodos are
   - Ⓐ endangered.
   - Ⓑ extinct.
   - Ⓒ polluted.
   - Ⓓ protected.

2. Which is **not** an example of pollution?

Ⓐ

Ⓑ

Ⓒ

Ⓓ

3. Why do you think a type of animal would become endangered if they don't have enough babies?

____

____

____

How Animals Become Endangered

Name: ____

Sometimes a type of animal becomes endangered. That means that type of animal is in danger of dying off completely. There would be no more of this type of animal if that happens.

How could something like that happen? Here are a few ways:

A. A type of animal could lose its habitat very quickly. A habitat is the place where an animal lives and where its food sources live. This place is perfect for that type of animal. If suddenly that place is destroyed, the animal may have no place to live and no food to eat.

B. A type of animal may be hunted too much by humans. Humans hunt animals for food or for sport.

C. Animals are the victims of poaching. Poaching is when animals are killed or badly injured for parts of their bodies, such as their fur, skin, horns, or other body parts. People use these parts to make things.

D. Pollution, which is usually caused by humans, poisons the air and water where some animals live and eat. The air the animals breathe becomes dangerous. The food they eat becomes bad for their health.

Directions: Read each true story about a type of animal that is endangered. Decide which reason above tells why that animal is in danger. Write the letter— **A**, **B**, **C**, or **D** — of the reason on the line.

________ **1.** **Green sea turtles** are in danger. In some countries, their meat and their eggs are eaten by people.

________ **2.** The number of **giant pandas** is growing smaller. Many of the forests they live in have been cut down.

________ **3.** The horn of the **black rhinoceros** is very valuable in some countries. The animals are killed, and their horns are used to make knife handles and medicine.

________ **4.** About 98% of the land that **brown spider monkeys** lived on is gone. Over 80% of the animals have died.

________ **5.** People use chemicals to kills insects and protect their crops. These chemicals get into the streams and poison the fish that **bald eagles** eat. This harms the eagles and their eggs.

Warm-Up 64

The Mystery of the "Terrible Lizards"

Name: ______________________________

Long ago, a group of animals ruled Earth. Some were the largest things on Earth. They weighed hundreds of thousands of pounds. Some were just the size of small birds. Some were hunters that ate meat. Others ate only plants. Some were fierce and deadly. That may be why we call this whole group of animals "dinosaurs." The word *dinosaur* means "terrible lizard."

Then, something happened. About 66 million years ago, most dinosaurs disappeared from Earth. Almost all of them died out. Only the ones who were most like birds lived.

How did this happen? No one knows for sure. Scientists can only make guesses from the information they have. Scientists think that one of these things happened:

- A large *meteorite* (an object from space) crashed into Earth. This changed the weather so much that dinosaurs could not survive.
- Large volcanoes erupted. The gas and the ash from the explosion made it too hard for the dinosaurs to breathe.
- A disease may have spread among the dinosaurs and killed them.

Directions: Follow these directions to show what you have learned about dinosaurs.

- On the dinosaur, write the meaning of the word "dinosaur."
- Next to the dinosaur, draw a volcano with lava coming out of it.
- Above the dinosaur, write the name of the object from space that may have crashed into Earth long ago.

The Last Ones of Their Kind

Warm-Up 65

Name: ______________________________

Some animals have gone extinct. This means that there are no more of them. Some animals, such as dinosaurs, went extinct a long time ago. Other animals were declared extinct very recently.

Directions: Use the clues to help you match each extinct animal with the year it went extinct. The first one has been done for you.

Clues

- The western black rhinoceros was declared extinct only a few years ago.
- The golden toad was declared extinct in 1989.
- The Caribbean monk seal was declared extinct 100 years after the great auk was.
- The quagga was like a zebra. It lasted only until the late 1800s.
- The dodo was declared extinct about 250 years before the passenger pigeon was.

	Animal	Year
	**Caribbean monk seal**	**1662**
	**dodo** (matched to 1662)	**1852**
	**golden toad**	**1883**
	**great auk**	**1914**
	**passenger pigeon**	**1952**
	**quagga**	**1989**
	**western black rhinoceros**	**2011**

Warm-Up 66

Fossils: Clues About the Past

Name: ______________________________

Some animals disappeared a long time ago. They disappeared before there were cameras or written words or even people! So how do we know so much about them?

One way we know so much is because we have found fossils. Fossils are clues. They teach us about the past. Sometimes a fossil is a bone. Sometimes it is a footprint. We can learn a lot about a living thing from a fossil it has left behind. We can learn about its size and shape. We can tell how long ago it lived.

Most living things do not leave behind fossils. Most parts of dead animals don't last very long. Other animals usually eat them, or the weather breaks them down. A lot of things have to happen for a fossil to survive for such a long time.

First, an animal has to die in the right place. It has to die in a place where the weather and other animals can't get to it easily. It needs to become buried.

Over time, rocks need to form above the animal. This pushes it down further and further below the surface. This protects it more. Deep down in the ground, minerals get into the animal's body. They help keep the shape of the animal and its parts. Even down there, a fossil won't last forever. Someone needs to come along and dig it up. Someone needs to find it.

Directions: Read each step about how fossils are made. Put the steps in order.

- Put a **1** next to the step that must come first.
- Put a **5** next to the step that comes last.

_______ Minerals get into the buried animal's body.

_______ A dead animal becomes buried beneath the surface.

_______ Someone finds the fossil of an animal that died long ago.

_______ An animal dies in a place where animals can't eat it.

_______ Rocks form above a buried animal. They push it further under the surface.

Which Fossil Did You Find?

Name: ______________________________

We have learned about creatures we have never seen. How did we do this? We learned about them from fossils.

Fossils can be body parts like bones, teeth, and shells. A fossil can be a footprint that never filled in. A fossil can even be a whole insect that got stuck in a sticky substance. That substance hardened, and the insect was trapped.

Directions: Look at each picture. Write what kind of fossil each one is.

bone	footprint	insect	shell	tooth

1.

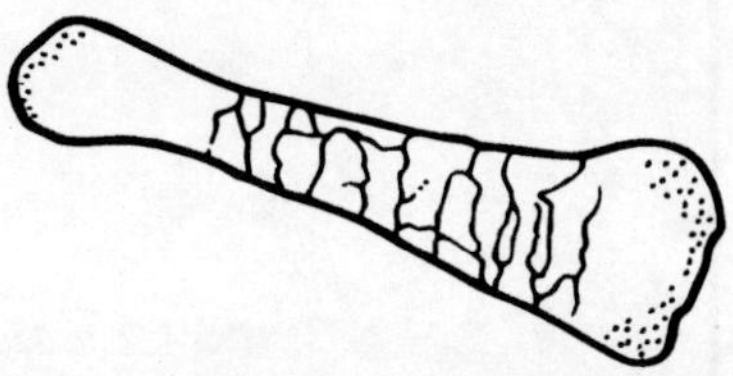

____

2.

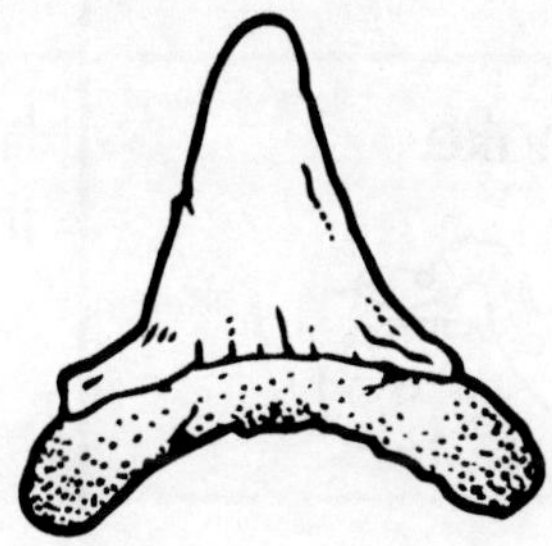

____

3.

____

4.

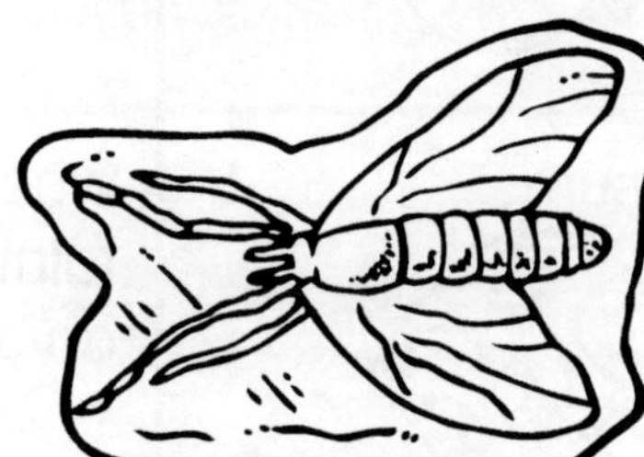

____

5.

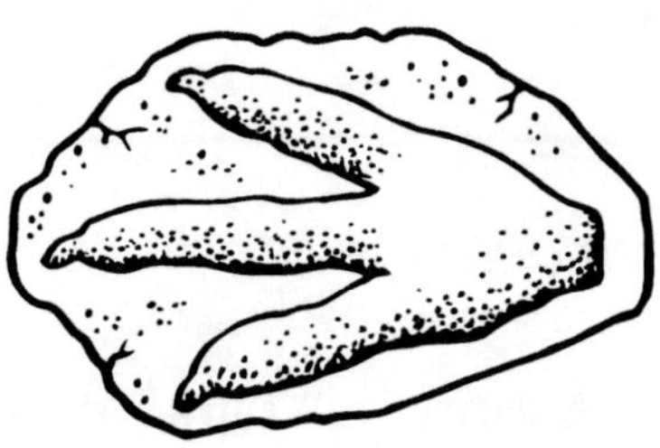

____

6.

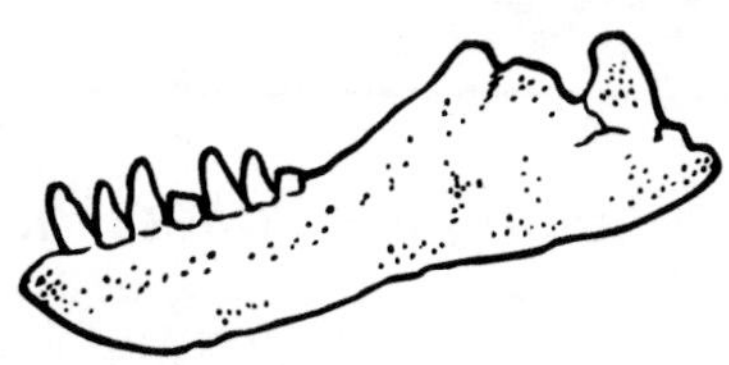

____

Warm-Up 68

Surviving in the Wild

Name: ______________________________

The wild is a dangerous place. Survival is hard for animals. Sometimes, an entire type of animal is in danger of dying out. So how do animals protect themselves? How do some types of animals live on while others die out?

Directions: Look at the chart below. Each of these animals has something special that helps them survive. These special things are called *adaptations*. Think about each animal's adaptation. How does it help them survive? Use the answers at the bottom of the page to help you complete the chart.

Animal	Adaptation	How It Helps Them Survive
1. rattlesnake 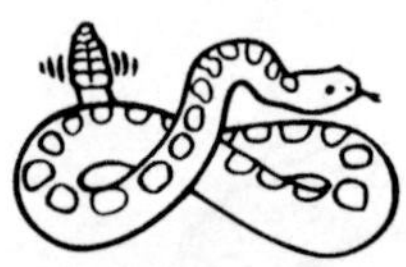	has a loud rattle on the end of its tail	
2. puffer fish 	can quickly fill its stomach with lots of water or air	
3. opossum 	when attacked, it faints and releases an awful scent	
4. monarch butterfly 	when young, it feeds on poisonous milkweed plants	

Cut these out along the dotted lines. Tape or glue them onto the chart.

It can suddenly look as if it is much bigger than it really is.	The food they eat makes them taste terrible to other animals.	The scary sound warns other animals to stay away.	Other creatures think this animal is dead, so they leave it alone.

Warm-Up 69

Name: ______________________________________

The names of dinosaurs often begin or end with the same letters. Many end in –*saurus*, for example. You can tell something about these dinosaurs by their names. Each part of their names means something.

Directions: Study the word beginnings and endings in the box. Then match the dinosaurs below to their names. The first one has been done for you.

Beginnings	Endings
Ovi- means "egg"	-*ceratops* means "horned head"
Pterano- means "winged"	-*raptor* means "thief"
Tri- means "three"	-*saurus* means "lizard"
Tyranno- means "terrible"	
Veloci- means "speedy"	

"winged lizard" — *Oviraptor* 

"terrible lizard" — *Pteranosaurus* 

"three-horned head" — *Tyrannosaurus* 

"egg thief" — *Triceratops* 

"speedy thief" — *Velociraptor* 

Warm-Up 70

The Important Lives of Plants

Name: ______________________________________

Plants come in all shapes and sizes. Think of a very tall tree. It is a plant. Think of any flower, fruit, vegetable, or nut. All of these come from plants.

Plants are living things. In many ways, they are like us. Just like us, they start out very small and then get bigger. Just like us, they need food to live and to grow.

Unlike us, plants can make their own food. How do they do this? They need a lot of help from sunlight and water.

Plants take energy from the sun and change it into food. They use a process called **photosynthesis** to do this. This process is very important to plants. It is also very important to everyone who lives on Earth. During photosynthesis, plants produce oxygen. They release oxygen into the air. People and other animals need oxygen to breathe. Thank you, plants!

What Did You Learn ?

1. Which of these is **not** a living thing?

Ⓐ house
Ⓑ tree
Ⓒ fish
Ⓓ plant

2. Which of these comes from a plant?

Ⓐ apple
Ⓑ cheese
Ⓒ peanut
Ⓓ both A and C

3. Who needs oxygen in order to live?

Ⓐ elephants
Ⓑ spiders
Ⓒ dolphins
Ⓓ answers A, B, and C

What Am I ?

I am the important process that plants use to make their own food. (Put one letter in each space to spell out the answer. A few letters have been written in for you.)

___ h ___ ___ o ___ ___ ___ t ___ ___ ___ ___ ___

We Need Each Other

Name: ______________________________

Did you know that you need plants, and they need you? It's true. When you breathe out, you release carbon dioxide. Plants need this to grow. As plants grow, they release oxygen. You need oxygen to breathe.

Directions: Look at the picture below.

- In **Arrow #1**, write what you give to trees to help them grow.
- In **Arrow #2**, write what trees give to you to help you breathe.

Use the **Word Bank** to help you spell the words.

Word Bank

oxygen
carbon dioxide

Warm-Up 72

The Basic Parts of a Plant

Name: ______________________________

A plant has many parts that work together. These parts help it live and grow.

Directions: Look at the picture of the big flower. Name the parts. Use the **Word Box** to help you. The first letter of each flower part is given for you.

Word Box

roots
stem
leaf
flower

1. This part is usually colorful. Its color and smell attract birds and bees. Those animals take pollen and share it with other plants.

f__ __ __ __ __ __

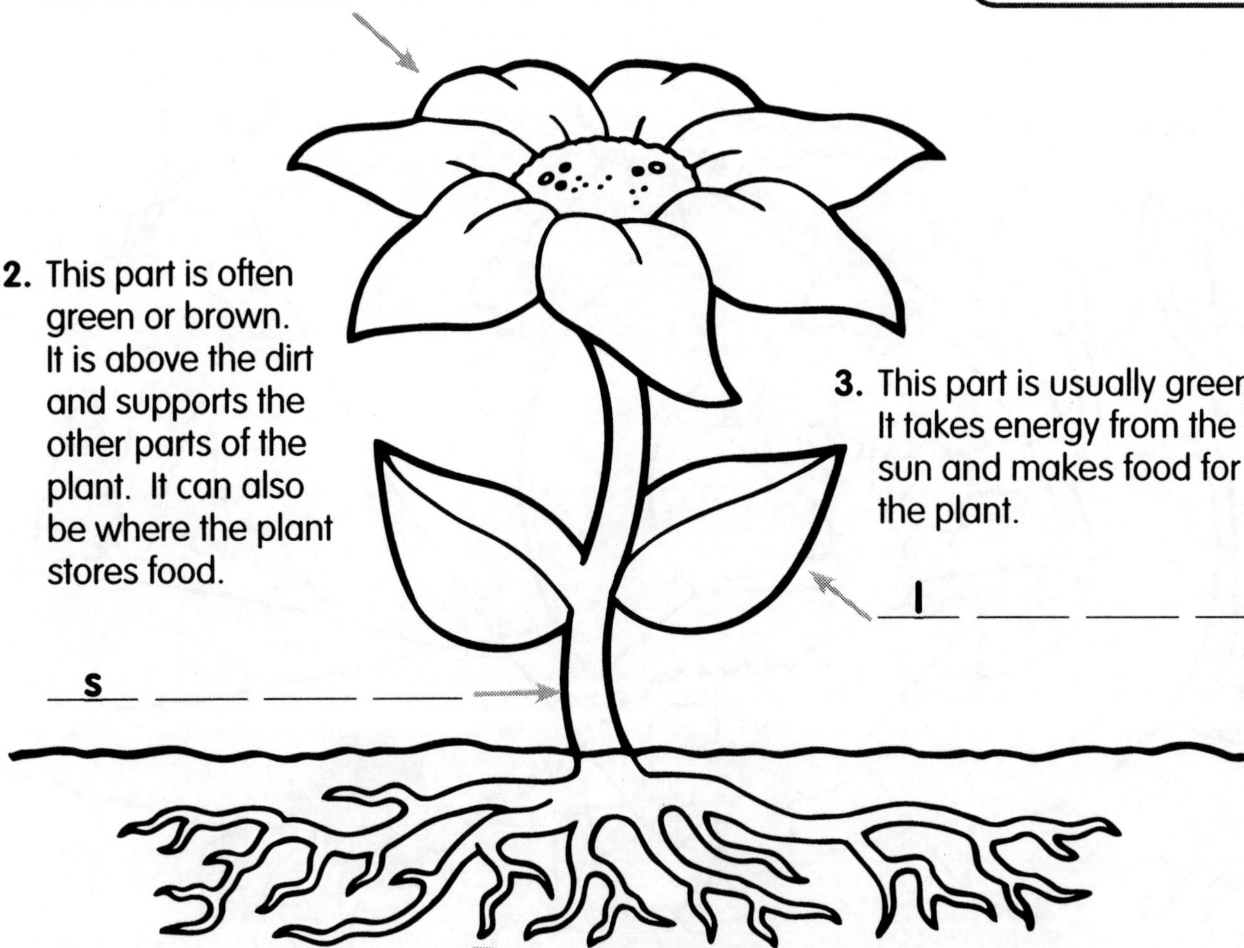

2. This part is often green or brown. It is above the dirt and supports the other parts of the plant. It can also be where the plant stores food.

s__ __ __ __

3. This part is usually green. It takes energy from the sun and makes food for the plant.

l__ __ __ __

4. These parts are under the dirt. They support the plant and bring nutrients from the soil to the plant.

r__ __ __ __ __

Plant Parts on Our Plates

Name: ______________________________

We eat fruits like apples and oranges and berries. Fruits come from plants. We eat other parts of plants, too.

Directions: Look at each picture of food that we eat. Which part of the plant do we eat? Write the plant part on the line. Use the words from the **Plant Parts** box.

Plant Parts	
flower	root
fruit	seeds
leaf	

1.

____

2.

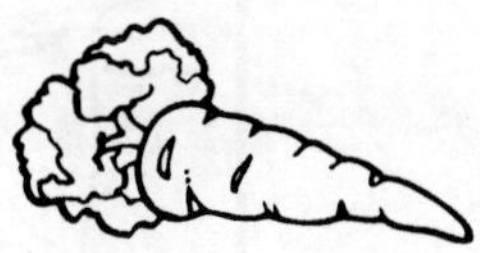

____

3.

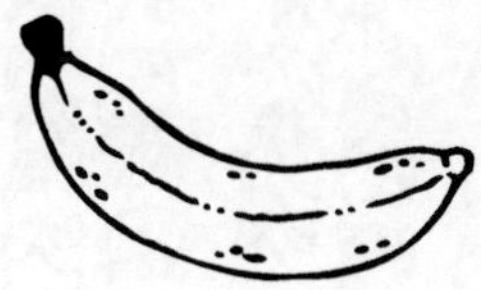

____

4.

____

5.

____

6.

____

7.

____

8.

____

9.

____

Warm-Up 74

A Plant's Life

Name: ______________________________

We can help plants grow. We can put seeds into the ground. We can give the seeds water and make sure they get plenty of sun. The plants grow bigger and bigger. We get a lot of food this way.

Directions: Look at the pictures below. They show a plant's life, but they are out of order! Number them in the order they should go. Put a **1** by the picture that shows what happens first. Put a **6** by the picture that shows what happens last.

 ________	 ________
 ________	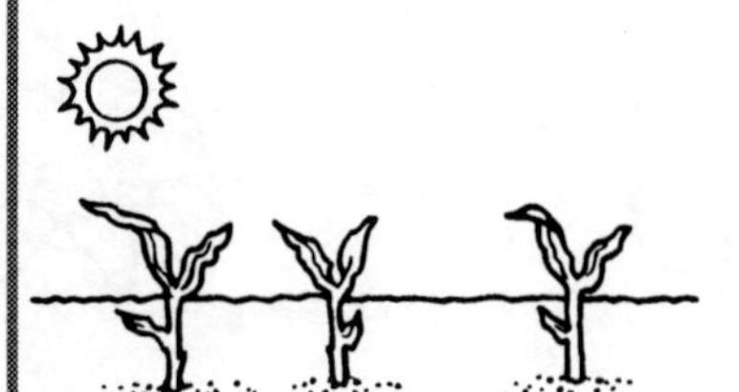 ________
 ________	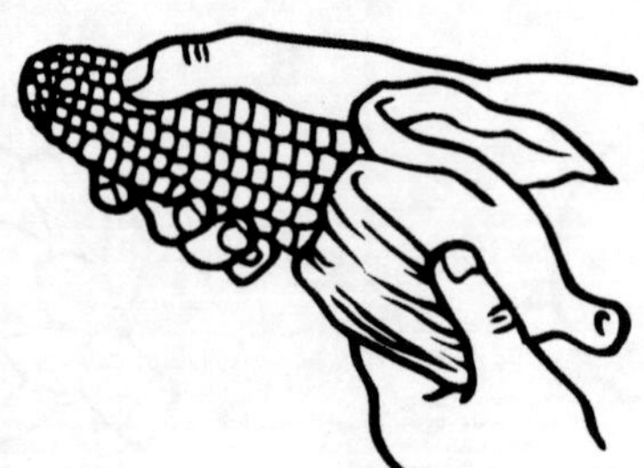 ________

Comparing Apples to Oranges

Name: ______________________________________

You have probably eaten both apples and oranges. Would you say that these two fruits are very alike or very different? Let's take a closer look.

First, let's think about how these fruits look. You have probably seen apples that are red, green, or yellow on the outside. They are white on the inside. Have you seen a ripe orange that isn't orange? There is one orange — called a blood orange — that is dark red inside.

What about the outside of the fruit? Apples are covered in a thin skin that is delicious and nutritious to eat. The rind of an orange is tough and thick.

Both fruits have seeds and both grow on trees. Apples, however, can grow in cold weather. Oranges need warm weather to grow.

Directions: Look at the diagram and the questions below it. In which part of the diagram would each sentence fit? On the line next to each sentence, write the letter of that part. The first one has been done for you.

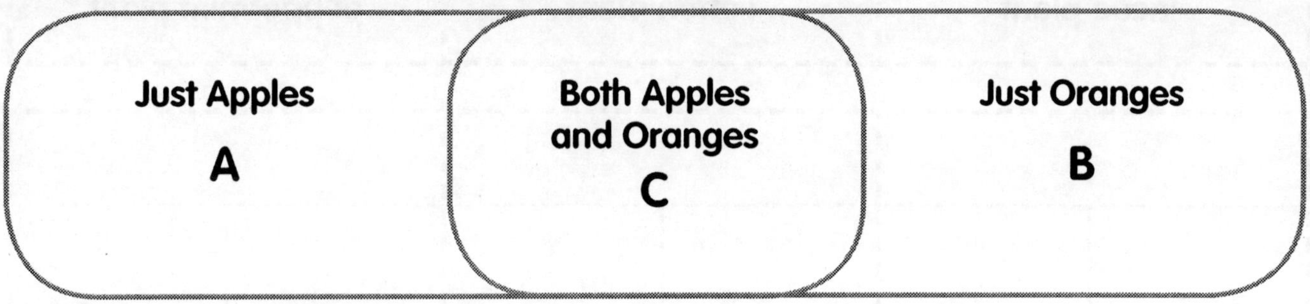

____C____ **1.** This fruit grows on trees.

_________ **2.** This fruit has seeds.

_________ **3.** This fruit is covered with a tough, thick rind.

_________ **4.** This fruit is covered by a thin skin you can eat.

_________ **5.** This fruit can grow in cold weather.

_________ **6.** This fruit can be green when it is ripe.

_________ **7.** This fruit can be orange.

_________ **8.** This fruit can be red inside.

Warm-Up 76

T-Shirts and Ketchup and So Much More

Name: ______________________________

We use plants every day. Many useful things come from plants.

Directions: Cut apart the boxes on the dashed lines. Match the name of the plant with the pictures of the products that are made from it.

Hint: There are two products for every plant.

Teacher Note: Have students glue the product pictures onto the plant cards.

cacao plant	cotton plant	peppermint plant
tomato plant	tree	wheat

'Tis the Season to Lose Leaves

Name: ____________________________________

Some trees lose their leaves each season. These trees are called *deciduous* trees. Their leaves start to fall off in the autumn (fall) months. By winter, these trees have almost no leaves.

Directions: Think about each date given below. Would that day be in the summer or spring? Or would it be in the winter or fall? Circle the picture that shows how a deciduous tree would most likely look on that day of the year.

Remember . . .

- Trees are full of leaves in the spring and summer.
- Trees are losing their leaves in the winter and fall.

1. December 16

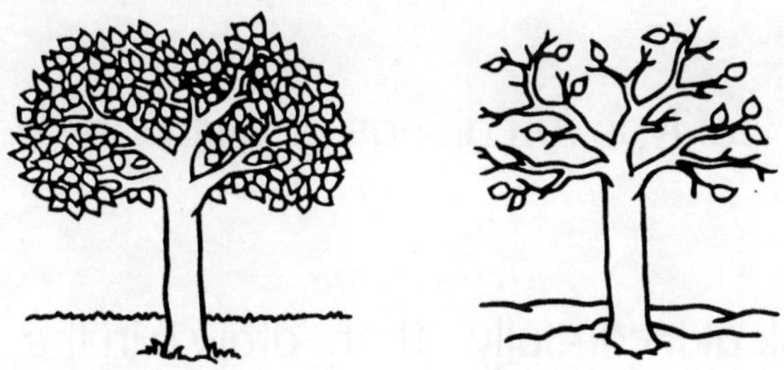

2. May 12

3. November 22

4. April 28

5. July 13

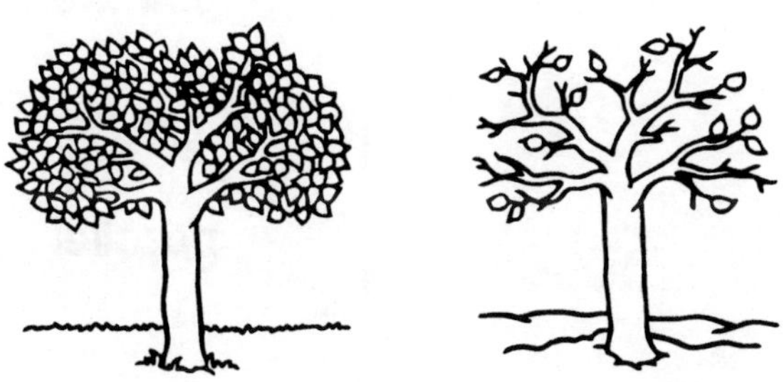

6. January 9

Warm-Up 78

Which of the Three Do You See?

Name: ______________________________

Have you ever looked at a leaf? Most have lines in them that you can see. These lines are called *veins.* They carry the water and other nutrients the plant needs.

There are three main vein types to look for:

palmate

The veins branch out from near the stem of the leaf. These leaves look almost like the palm of your hand.

pinnate

These leaf types often have a main vein. Sometimes it goes down the middle of the leaf.

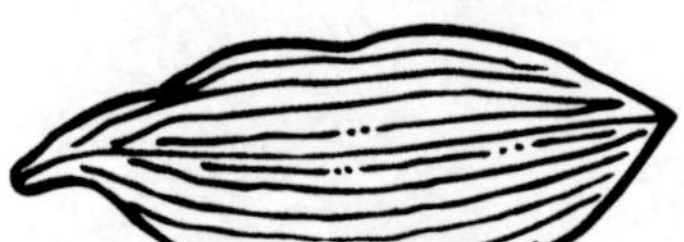

parallel

The veins in this leaf type run alongside each other in straight lines.

Directions: Find a clean leaf from outside. Look at it carefully. Then, draw it in the box below. Be sure to draw the veins and the stem of the leaf. After you have finished, circle what kind of vein type your leaf is. Is it palmate, pinnate, or parallel?

Circle one.

palmate

pinnate

parallel

Warm-Up 79

Name: ______________________________

Trees can be used in many ways. The fruit from some trees can be used for food. The wood can be used to build things. Trees also provide shade for us, and they provide homes for many animals.

Some words can also be used in many ways. Some words can mean more than one thing.

Example:

The outer covering of a tree is called **bark**.
I heard our dog **bark** at the mailman.

Directions: Each sentence below is missing a word. Use a tree word from the box to complete the sentence.

Tree Words		
branch	rings	stump
leaves	roots	trunk

1. Bob is a fan of the soccer team. He ____________________ for them to win every game.

2. How will you move the piano? It won't fit in the ____________________ of your car.

3. Emma is always in a hurry. She often ____________________ before the movie is over.

4. Mr. Shell needs to fix the school bell. It ____________________ too loudly and for too long.

5. I can't figure out the answer to the riddle. Did it ____________________ you, too?

6. Let's not go there again. We should ____________________ out and visit new places.

Warm-Up 80

All Systems Go!

Name: ____

The human body is an amazing machine. It is made up of many parts that work together. We can't see most of these parts, but they are always working. Some of these parts form groups called *systems*. For example, all of your muscles work together to form the *muscular system*. The parts of this system help us move our whole body and also little parts of it. Did you know that it takes a total of 17 muscles to smile? All 17 muscles work together without our even knowing it. Even more incredibly, it takes 42 muscles to frown!

Your body has 10 systems in total. One system includes all of your bones. It is called the *skeletal system*. Another system works to help you breathe. It is called the *respiratory system*. It includes such parts as your nose, throat, windpipe, and lungs. The *digestive system* includes your mouth, stomach, and intestines. Can you guess what this system helps you do?

What Did You Learn ?

1. A group of parts working together is called a

Ⓐ muscle. Ⓑ total. Ⓒ system.

2. The bones in your arms and legs would be a part of which system?

Ⓐ muscular Ⓑ skeletal Ⓒ respiratory

3. Your digestive system is most needed to help you

Ⓐ eat. Ⓑ run. Ⓒ dance.

4. Look at the symbols in the box. Which one would you use to complete the sentence? Write the symbol on the line.

$<$ means "is less than"	$=$ means "is equal to"
$>$ means "is greater than"	

the number of muscles needed to smile ____________ the number of muscles needed to frown

Your Hard-Working Heart

Name: ______________________________

You have many muscles in your body. Muscles make things move. Your most important muscle may be your heart. It is always working. What does it move? It moves blood through your body. Your heart is like a pump. Really, it is like two pumps.

There are two sides to your heart. They are called the left heart and the right heart. Blood from your body flows into your right heart. This blood is low in oxygen and nutrients. Those things have been used up by your body. Your right heart takes this blood and pumps it into your lungs. The blood picks up oxygen there. This blood with oxygen in it then flows into your left heart. Your left heart pumps this blood out to your brain and to the rest of your body. After that blood is used, it is sent back to your right heart. This happens over and over again. Special parts called *valves* make sure that blood always flows in the correct direction.

Directions: Look at each diagram. Follow the arrows. They show the direction that blood flows. Fill in the circle next to each best answer.

1. Blood from body → right heart →

Ⓐ is full of oxygen

Ⓑ needs oxygen

2. Blood from right heart → the lungs →

Ⓐ goes to left heart

Ⓑ goes to body

3. Blood from lungs → left heart →

Ⓐ goes to brain

Ⓑ goes to right heart

What Am I ?

I make sure blood from your heart never flows the wrong way. I am a . . .

___ ___ ___ ___ ___

Warm-Up 82

Are You in Your Right Mind?

Name: ______________________________

The brain is divided into two halves. These halves work together. For some things that you do, however, one half is more active than the other. The diagram below tells the story.

Left Side of the Brain
speaking
reading
controlling the right side of the body

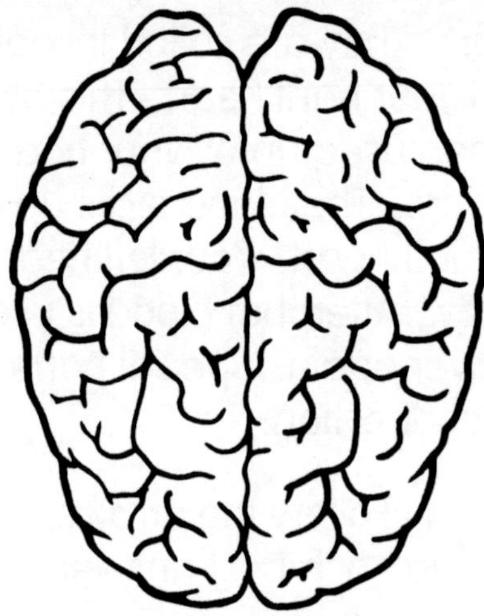

Right Side of the Brain
recognizing faces
drawing pictures
controlling the left side of the body

Directions: It's time to use your whole brain … concentrating on one half at a time!

On the Left Side

Write about a time outside of school when you needed to talk your way out of a difficult situation.

____

____

____

____

____

____

____

____

____

On the Right Side

Draw a picture of the difficult situation you just wrote about.

With a Little Help from Your Friend

Name: ______________________________

Your skeleton supports your body and helps you move. It protects your brain, heart, and other organs. Your skeleton is a good friend to have!

Directions: Read each question. Circle the answer you think is correct. If you get it wrong, your friend will lend you a hand in finding the answer.

1. Where is the longest bone in your body located?

   Circle your answer: *your leg* *your arm* *your neck*

"Give yourself a standing ovation if you got this one right! The longest bone is called the *femur*, and it is in your upper leg. Your femur is very long and incredibly strong."

2. Where is the smallest bone in your body located?

   Circle your answer: *your mouth* *your ear* *your pinkie toe*

"Listen up and hear, and you will use your smallest bone to do so! You have three tiny bones in your ear, and the smallest is called the *stapes*. It is shaped like a little horseshoe."

3. Who has the most bones?

   Circle your answer: *an adult* *a teenager* *a baby*

"Could you count to 350 when you were born? That's about how many bones you had back then. Some were soft, and some grew together as you got older. By the time you are an adult, you will have exactly 206 bones."

Think About It! Which skeleton fact surprised you the most? Why?

____

____

____

Warm-Up 84

Three of Each

Name: ______________________________

Here are some facts about the human body:

- There are three main parts of the brain: the cerebrum, the cerebellum, and the brain stem.
- There are three bones in the human ear: the malleus, the incus, and the stapes.
- There are three main leg bones: the femur, the tibia, and the fibula.
- There are three bones in the human arm: the humerus, the radius, and the ulna.
- There are three types of baby teeth: incisors, canines, and molars.

Part 1 Directions: Look at the name of the body part on the left. Draw a line to connect it to the place where it can be found in your body.

tibia

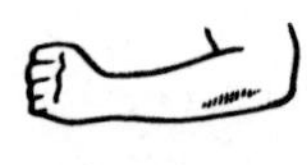

molar

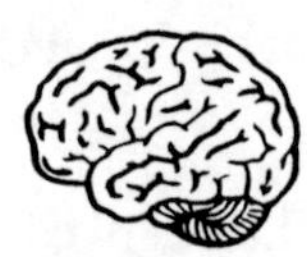

cerebellum

radius

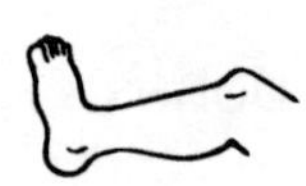

incus

Part 2 Directions: Look at the skeleton. Two of the arm bones are given. Write the name of the third arm bone.

____

radius

ulna

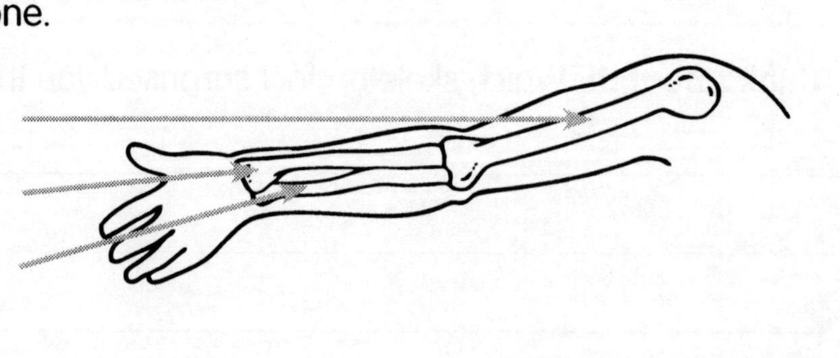

Making Sense of Your Senses

Name: ______________________________

Humans have five main senses:

the sense of **SIGHT**

the sense of **TASTE**

the sense of **HEARING**

the sense of **TOUCH**

the sense of **SMELL**

Directions: Read each object or idea. Write down the sense you first think of for each one. Write **SIGHT**, **HEARING**, **SMELL**, **TASTE**, or **TOUCH** on the line next to the object or idea.

1. a soft blanket ______________________________
2. an ice-cream cone ______________________________
3. loud music ______________________________
4. bright colors ______________________________
5. freshly baked bread ______________________________
6. a hot oven ______________________________
7. a shiny toy ______________________________
8. a barking dog ______________________________
9. bacon frying ______________________________
10. a waterfall ______________________________

Now look back at each answer you gave. Is there another answer you could have given? For each one, try to write down another sense that you would also use.

Warm-Up 86

What Happens in the Blink of an Eye

Name: ______________________________

Have you ever thought about how often you blink? Have you ever tried to count how many times you blink? Is blinking something we need to do? Yes, it is!

- It provides moisture to the surface of your eyeball. If there is not enough moisture, your eye will feel dried out.
- It helps keep your eye clean. Tiny pieces of dust and other things land on the surface of your eyes all of the time. Your eyelids' up-and-down motion wipes these things away.

Most people blink about 15 times per minute. This number can be larger or smaller for many reasons. One reason is age. Very young babies only blink once or twice per minute. Their eyes don't need as much moisture. Someone who is looking at a computer also blinks less. A person using a computer might only blink seven times per minute. This is one reason why your eyes might get tired and more dried out if you use the computer for a long time.

Directions: Finish filling in the chart. Write the number of blinks in each box. Use the completed chart to answer the questions below.

Number of Minutes	1	2	3	4	5	10
Average Person	15	30	45		75	150
Young Baby	2		6		10	
Computer User	7	14		28		70

1. How many times does the average person blink in 2 minutes?

Ⓐ 30 Ⓑ 20 Ⓒ 15 Ⓓ 10

2. How many times does a young baby blink in 10 minutes?

Ⓐ 4 Ⓑ 10 Ⓒ 20 Ⓓ 40

3. Who would blink most?

Ⓐ a young baby in 10 minutes
Ⓑ a computer user in 4 minutes
Ⓒ the average person in 2 minutes

A Matter of Taste

Name: ______________________________

It can take great teamwork to get a job done well. When it comes to taste, your tongue and your nose work as a team.

Your tongue has thousands of tiny bumps on it. These are called taste buds. When you put food in your mouth, those taste buds send messages to your brain. They tell your brain if the food is sweet, sour, bitter, or salty. But that's not the whole story when it comes to taste. You also have special cells inside your nose. The messages from your tongue pass by these cells. These cells give your brain even more information about food's flavor.

Have you ever noticed that you can't taste food as well when your nose is stuffy? That's because the cells in your nose are blocked. You might still be able to tell if your food is sweet, sour, bitter, or salty, but you can't get the rest of the flavor.

You might also notice that hot food is tastier than cold food. That's because hot food releases a larger amount of chemicals into the air than cold food. The cells in your nose smell more of the food, so the food seems to have more taste.

Part 1 Directions: Fill in the circle next to each correct answer.

1. Which diagram shows the direction information flows when you taste food?

Ⓐ brain → nose → mouth

Ⓑ mouth → brain → nose

Ⓒ mouth → nose → brain

2. Which would release the *least* amount of chemicals into the air?

Ⓐ warm bread Ⓑ cold pizza Ⓒ hot soup

Part 2 Directions: The story tells of four types of tastes that your tongue can find. Find and circle all four in the puzzle below.

T A L T Y S O

S E U R M W L

O B I T T E R

U S L A E E K

R P S A L T Y

What Gives You Goose Bumps?

Name: ________________________________

Your skin is very important. It protects the inside of your body from the outside world. It allows you to sweat when you are too hot. What does it do when you are too cold? It gives you goose bumps, and that is a good thing!

Goose bumps are what we call those bumps on your skin when you are cold. They are caused when the hair on your body stands straight up. This helps trap a layer of warm air next to your skin. It helps you save your body's heat. Tiny muscles under your skin do this. They pull the hair up. This causes the skin around each hair to bunch up. Your skin then looks like it is covered in bumps.

Part 1 Directions: Read the statements below. They explain how you get goose bumps, but they are not in the correct order. Put a number on the line to show what order they should be in. Put a **1** next to the event that happens first. Put a **2** next to the event that happens next, and so on.

_______ The skin around your hairs bunches up.

_______ Tiny muscles under your skin pull your hairs up.

_______ Your skin looks like it is covered in bumps.

_______ A cold breeze blows across your skin.

Part 2 Directions: You don't get goose bumps just when you are cold. People and animals can also get them when they feel a very strong emotion, such as fear. For some animals, they raise their hair to look bigger. This scares away other animals who are trying to harm them. Circle the animal below who is showing this response.

Why Your Foot Takes a Nap

Name: ______________________________

Has your foot ever fallen asleep? This usually happens when you sit for a long time with your foot tucked under you. Then, when you try to straighten your leg out, your foot feels strange. It tingles. It doesn't work very well. You might say, "My foot fell asleep!"

You have nerves running throughout your body. Nerves are like threads or wires. They carry messages back and forth between your brain and your body. If you touch something hot, your nerves will send a message to your brain. Your brain will get the message, "Hot! Remove hand now!" Then, you remove your hand from the hot object. This happens very quickly. This helps protect you from getting really hurt.

When you sit on your foot for a long time, you put too much weight on the nerves in that area. You squish them down. This cuts off the connection between the nerves and your brain. You have to get up and move around to get the connection back.

This doesn't last too long. You're not hurt in any way. Once you move around, the connection comes right back. But for a few seconds, your foot will tingle and it will feel as if it's asleep.

Directions: Write a paragraph. Choose one of these topics:

- Describe what it feels like when your foot falls asleep.
- Imagine that you have touched something that is really hot or really cold. What would your nerves and your brain say to each other?

____

____

____

____

____

____

____

Warm-Up 90

Things That Grow and Grow

Name: ______________________________

Your body is changing all of the time. You are growing. Some parts of you grow faster than other parts. Think about your hair. It grows about a half an inch each month. That means it grows about 6 inches each year.

Your fingernails and toenails also grow fast. But not all of these nails grow at the same speed. For example, the nails on your longer fingers grow faster than the nails on your shorter fingers. This means that the nail on your middle finger grows the fastest. The next fastest are your ring finger and your index finger. The nail on your thumb grows the slowest of all your fingernails. The time of year also is important. Your nails grow faster in the summertime than they do in the winter.

Most people cut their hair and their fingernails to keep them from growing too long. How long is your hair? How long are your fingernails? A man from India holds the record for the longest fingernail. He let the thumbnail on his left hand grow until it measured over 4 feet long! It curled around and around.

Directions: Answer each question.

1. According to the story, about how many inches would your hair grow in two years? ______________________

2. According to the story, during which month would your fingernails grow the slowest? (Circle your answer.)

March **July** **October** **December**

3. Look at the picture of the hand. Put a **1** on the nail that grows the fastest. Put a **5** on the nail that grows the slowest.

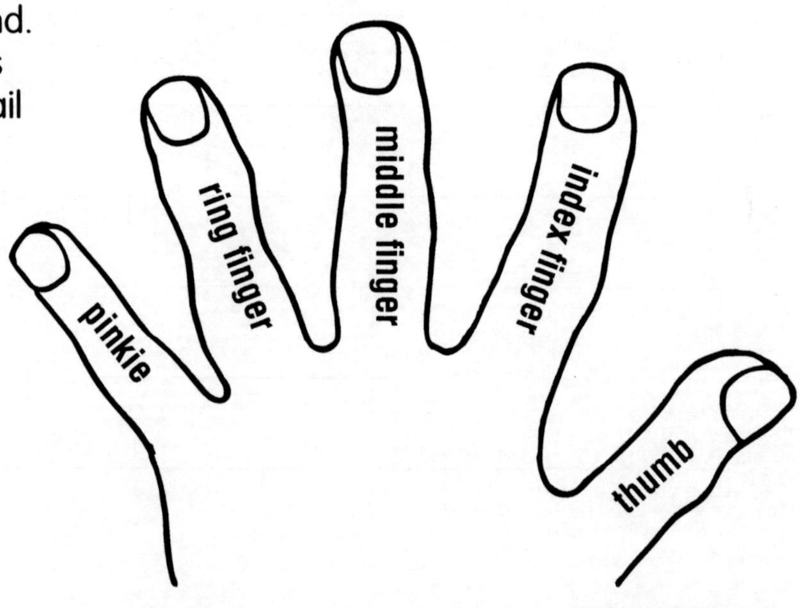

Warm-Up 91

Name: ____________________________________

Read this sentence. Can you see the body part that is hidden in it?

- There is one zebra in our city's zoo.

Can you see that the word *brain* is hidden in that sentence? Look again.

- There is one zebra in our city's zoo.

Part 1 Directions: Read each sentence. Search for a body part that is hidden. Circle the body part in each sentence. Use the **Parts Box** to help you.

Parts Box

ankle
finger
knee
mouth
nose
stomach
thumb

1. The sink needs to be washed.

2. Frank let us pet his dog.

3. This movie makes no sense!

4. She refuses to machine-wash her clothes.

5. Kay carries a cloth umbrella on sunny days.

6. Sonya lost her scarf in Germany last winter.

7. "Has anyone seen Jim out here?" asked Bob.

Part 2 Directions: Now try it yourself. Write a sentence that has these body parts hidden somewhere inside.

8. arm ____

9. leg ____

10. head ____

Warm-Up 92

The Importance of Good Health

Name: ______________________________

Your health is very important. It is what lets you play and think and sleep. You feel great when your body is healthy.

What can you do to stay healthy? There are many things you can do. You can eat good food and drink plenty of water. The vitamins and nutrients in food help your body do everything it needs to do.

You can also get good sleep and exercise. Exercise helps keep you from gaining unneeded weight, and it helps keep your body strong and **flexible**. Sleep and rest help your body get back the energy you used up during the day. It helps your body to heal and grow.

It is also important to wash your hands and to stay clean. Washing your hands keeps germs from getting into your body.

When you do get sick, it is important to see a doctor. Doctors know how our bodies work. They can tell us what we can do to get better.

What Did You Learn ?

1. Which one of these is **not** listed in the story as a way to be healthy?
   - Ⓐ eating good food
   - Ⓑ exercising
   - Ⓒ playing video games
   - Ⓓ getting good sleep

2. Washing your hands can help keep ______________ out of your body.
   - Ⓐ germs
   - Ⓑ nutrients
   - Ⓒ vitamins
   - Ⓓ energy

3. If you are flexible, you can bend and move easily. Which one of these people is being flexible?

Ⓐ

Ⓑ

Ⓒ

What Am I ?

I can help you get better when you are sick. I am a ___ o ___ ___ o ___.

Nature's Perfect Drink

Warm-Up 93

Name: ______________________________________

What will you drink with your dinner tonight? Just about the best thing you could do for your body is pour yourself a tall glass of water. It's nature's perfect drink.

Water helps your body do so many things. It carries oxygen to all the cells of your body. It helps you use the food that you eat. It helps you sweat when you run and play. It helps you get better when you are ill. This is why you need extra water when you are sick or when you exercise. Your body is working harder, and water helps it do that.

Water is not just in your glass. Many foods that you eat have a lot of water in them. Think of juicy fruits, like peaches and oranges. Vegetables are full of water, too.

Do you know what else is full of water? You! Over half of your body's weight comes from water. It's *that* important.

Directions: Circle the pictures that show the best answers.

1. All of these people need water. Circle the two who need the most water right now.

2. Which of these foods have the most water in them? Circle two.

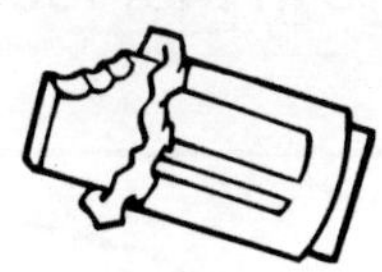

3. How much water do you drink each day? Do you think you get enough? Should you drink more? Write a few sentences about you and water.

____

____

____

____

Warm-Up 94

What's On Your Plate?

Name: ____________________________________

What you eat is called your diet. It is very important for you to have a healthy diet. There are five food groups that are the building blocks of a healthy diet.

Food Group	Examples
Vegetables	broccoli, spinach, carrots, corn, peas, onions, asparagus
Fruits	apples, oranges, bananas, berries, melons, raisins
Proteins	meat, fish, eggs, beans, nuts, tofu
Grains	bread, rice, pasta, cereal, oatmeal, crackers
Dairy	milk, yogurt, cheese

There is a nutrition guide called **MyPlate**. It is a picture of a plate. The plate shows the amounts you should eat from each food group. On MyPlate, the biggest amounts are vegetables and grains. Your diet should have a lot of vegetables and grains in it.

Directions: Look at the picture below. It is a picture of MyPlate. What would your plate look like? In each section, draw a picture of your favorite food. Make sure that the food you draw belongs in that food group.

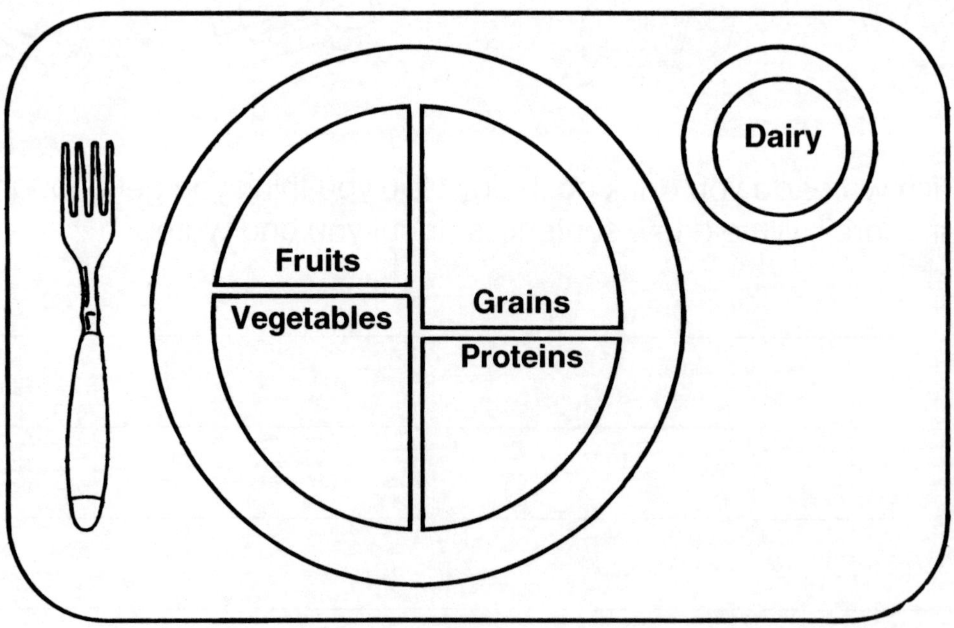

Burning Calories

Warm-Up 95

Name: ______________________________

A calorie is a measure of how much energy we get from food. We need calories to help us move, play, and think. If we take in (eat) too many calories and don't use them, we gain weight. When we use calories, we say that we are burning them.

We burn some calories even as we sit and read. But if we really want to burn calories, we need to move. Some activities burn more calories than others. The harder your body works, the more calories it burns.

Here is a graph that shows some popular activities and about how many calories each one burns per minute:

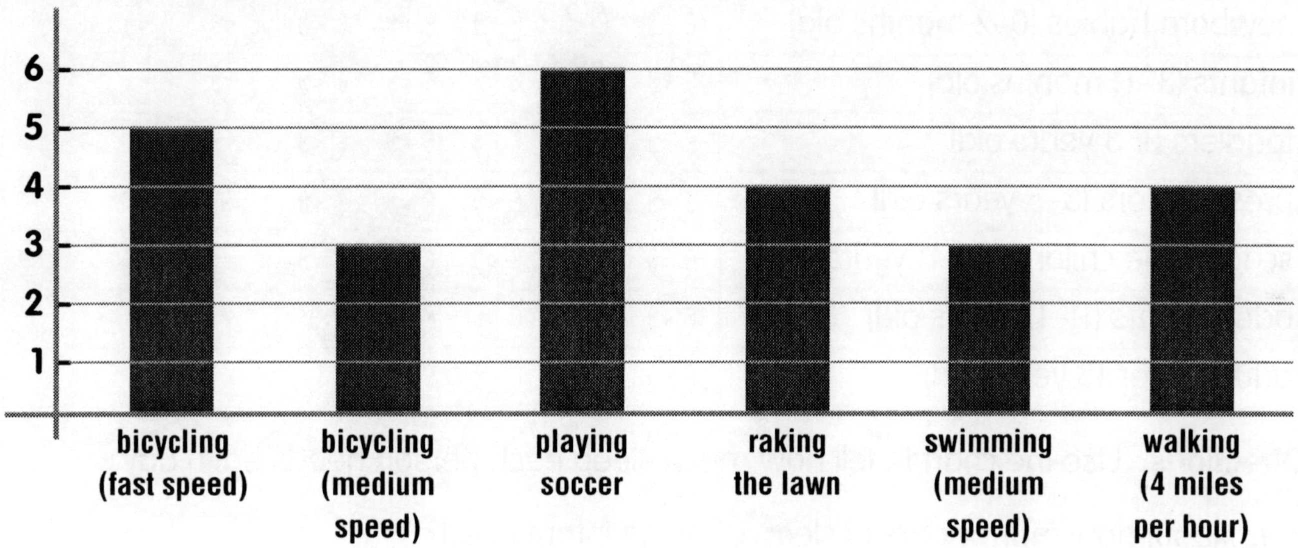

Directions: Use the graph to answer the following questions.

1. Which of these activities burns the most calories?

Ⓐ walking Ⓑ soccer Ⓒ raking

2. How many more calories per minute does bicycling fast burn than bicycling at a medium speed?

Ⓐ 1 Ⓑ 2 Ⓒ 3

3. If you raked the lawn for 10 minutes, about how many calories would you burn?

Ⓐ 10 Ⓑ 20 Ⓒ 40

Name 3! What are your favorite activities? List three. Circle the one that you think would burn the most calories.

______________________ ______________________ ______________________

Warm-Up 96

How Much Sleep Do You Need?

Name: ______________________________

We need to sleep. Getting good sleep is an important part of being healthy. Sleep helps us heal when we are sick or hurt. Without sleep, our minds and bodies don't work as well as they should.

Not all people need the same amount of sleep. Your age is one reason why you would need more or less sleep. Look at the chart. It shows about how much sleep each day that people of different ages need.

Key: = 2 hours = 1 hour

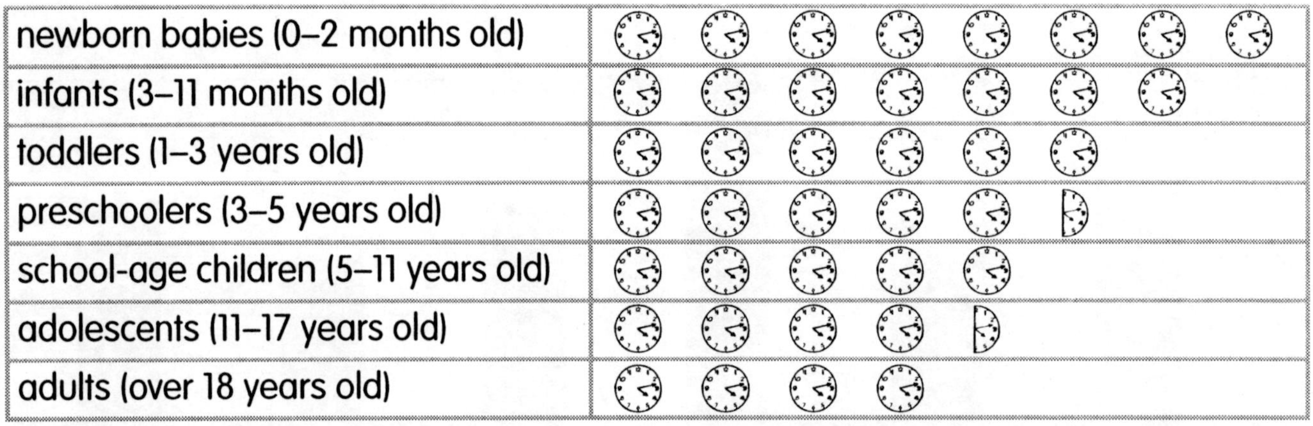

Directions: Use the chart to tell how much sleep each person needs each day.

1. About how many hours of sleep does an infant need? ______________
2. About how many hours of sleep does an adult need? ______________
3. About how many hours of sleep do you need? ______________
4. About how many fewer hours of sleep does an adolescent need than a toddler? (Fill in the circle next to the correct answer.)

   Ⓐ 1½ Ⓑ 3 Ⓒ 5

5. Look at these two statements. Circle the one that is true.

We need more sleep as we get older.

We need more sleep when we are younger.

Now tell why you think this might be true. (**Hint:** There are no wrong answers!)

____

____

Warm-Up 97

An Army on the Inside

Name: ______________________________________

You get sick sometimes. Everyone does. Germs get into your body and try to make you sick. Your body doesn't like that. It fights back. It releases an army to help fight the germs. This army defends you all day, every day. It protects you from getting really sick, and it helps you get better faster. This army is called your *immune system*.

You have white blood cells in your body. They are a big part of your immune system. White blood cells fight germs and break them up. They also remember germs they have fought before. This helps them keep you from getting the same sickness over and over again.

You also have lymph nodes. They are another part of your immune system. These nodes are groups of cells that help remove germs from of your body. You have lymph nodes in places like your neck, your armpits, and behind your knees. When you are sick, your doctor might feel your neck. Your doctor is checking to see if your lymph nodes are swollen (puffed out). This tells your doctor that your immune system is working hard to fight germs.

Part 1 Directions: Look at the person to the right. Circle three places on the person's body where lymph nodes can be found.

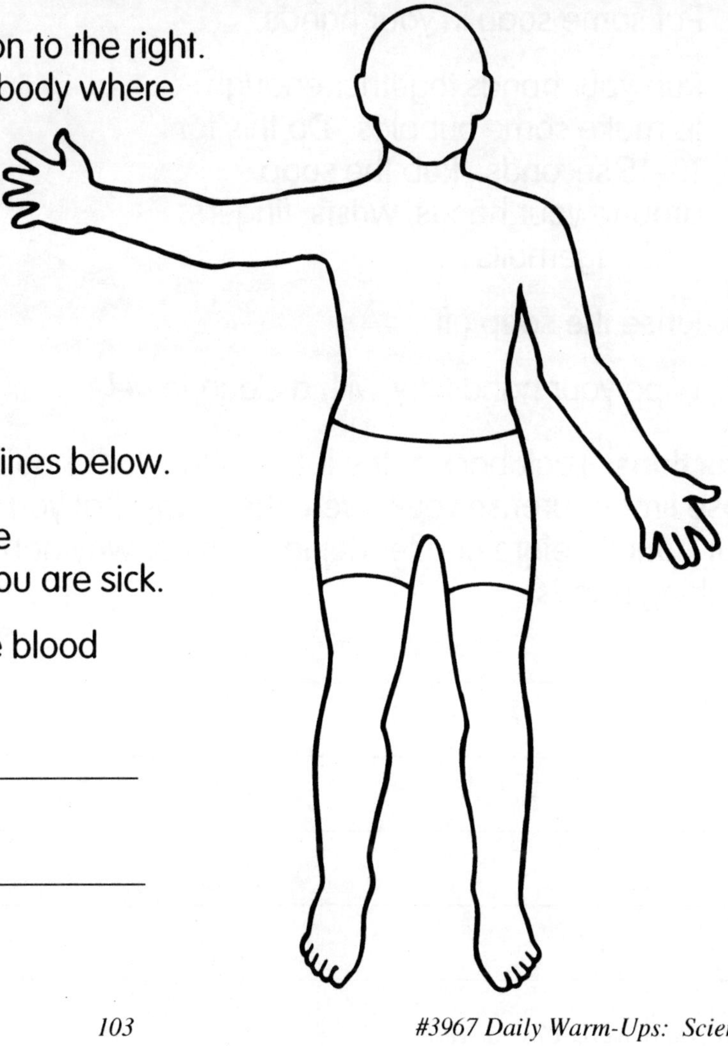

Part 2 Directions: Look at the two lines below.

- On Line 1, write the name of the army that protects you when you are sick.
- On Line 2, write the color of the blood cells that fight germs.

Line 1: ______________________________

Line 2: ______________________________

Soap + Water = Health

Name: ______________________________

There is one simple thing you can do to stop a lot of germs before they can make you sick. You can wash your hands. This one thing can often keep you from getting sick.

No one can (or should) wash their hands *all* of the time. When is it most important to wash them? You should wash them. . .

- when they look dirty.
- before you touch, make, or eat food.
- after you use the bathroom.
- after you blow your nose.
- after visiting a sick friend or relative.
- after playing outside.
- after you touch pets or animals.

Now that you know *when*, it's time to talk about *how* you should wash your hands. Here are some handy tips to remember:

1. Use warm water.
2. Put some soap in your hands.
3. Rub your hands together enough to make some bubbles. Do this for 10–15 seconds. Rub the soap around your hands, wrists, fingers, and fingernails.
4. Rinse the soap off.
5. Wipe your hands dry with a clean towel.

Directions: Look back at the list of when you should wash your hands. Did any of those times surprise you? Were there any that you thought you didn't need to wash your hands before or after doing? Why or why not? Write a few sentences about washing hands.

____

____

____

____

____

Warm-Up 99

Name: ______________________________

There are many parts to the human body. Every doctor can't be an expert on every part. That's why there are many different types of doctors. There are doctors who are experts in treating one part.

Each type of doctor has a name. You can tell what kind of doctor he or she is by the first part of that name.

Directions: Draw lines to match each name with the body part(s) that doctor treats. Use the **Clues Box** to help you. The first one is done for you.

Type of Doctor	Treats
1. audiologist	teeth
2. cardiologist	feet and ankles
3. dentist	ears and hearing
4. dermatologist	stomach
5. gastroenterologist	immune system
6. podiatrist	heart
7. immunologist	skin

Clues Box

The French word part *dent* means "tooth."

The Greek word part *gaster* means "stomach."

The Greek word part *derma* means "skin."

The Greek word part *pod* means "foot."

An *audio* tape is a recording of sound.

Muscle found in the heart is called *cardiac* muscle.

Warm-Up 100

A World Built on Ideas

Name: ______________________________

Scientists study our world. They look at the smallest things, like the cells in our bodies and the tiny viruses that make us sick. They also study the largest things, like outer space. They study everything in between. Without scientists, we wouldn't know why we get sick or why the sun rises and sets each day.

Inventors create new things. Some inventors are scientists. They have invented new medicines and new materials to make our lives easier and more comfortable. They have created new technology to entertain us and help us visit faraway lands.

Not all inventors are scientists, though. Some have just been regular people who have had good ideas and have worked hard to make their ideas come to life. We use their inventions every day.

Many older inventions have made newer inventions possible. Scientists and inventors use the idea of those who came before them. They improve older inventions and discoveries. They make them even better.

What Did You Learn ?

1. Scientists and inventors study the world. This gives them ideas. What did the inventors of airplanes probably study?

   Ⓐ the way fish swim
   Ⓑ the way birds fly
   Ⓒ the way horses run
   Ⓓ the way snakes crawl

2. Scientists and inventors learn from the work of others. Which event probably happened first?

   Ⓐ A tiny virus was discovered in a sick person's cells.
   Ⓑ A medicine was created to help people with the tiny virus.
   Ⓒ A microscope for looking at tiny things was invented.

3. Name an invention that makes your life better. Explain why it does. (There are no right or wrong answers to this question!)

   Invention: ______________________________

   Why it makes your life better: ______________________________

   ____

   ____

How Scientists Must Think

Name: ____

Scientists are curious. They like to solve puzzles, and they like to learn about new things. They have to be like detectives searching for clues in the world. By doing this, they can learn how the world works.

Scientists use something called the **scientific method**. This method is the way that scientists learn. They begin by asking a question about the world. The question may be something like, "Why is the sky blue?" or "Why are cheetahs so fast?" The scientist may have an idea what the answer is to this question. They cannot just guess at the answer, however. They must use the scientific method to find facts that help answer the question. They must be able to prove that their facts are true. How do they do this? They do experiments. They use their senses (seeing, hearing, smelling, touching, and tasting) to observe. When they find answers, they have to do more tests. They check their answers again and again. Scientists must be sure that their findings are correct.

Directions: Look at the web below. Color in the bubbles that show ways scientists learn more about things. Draw an **X** through the bubbles that do not show the scientific method being used.

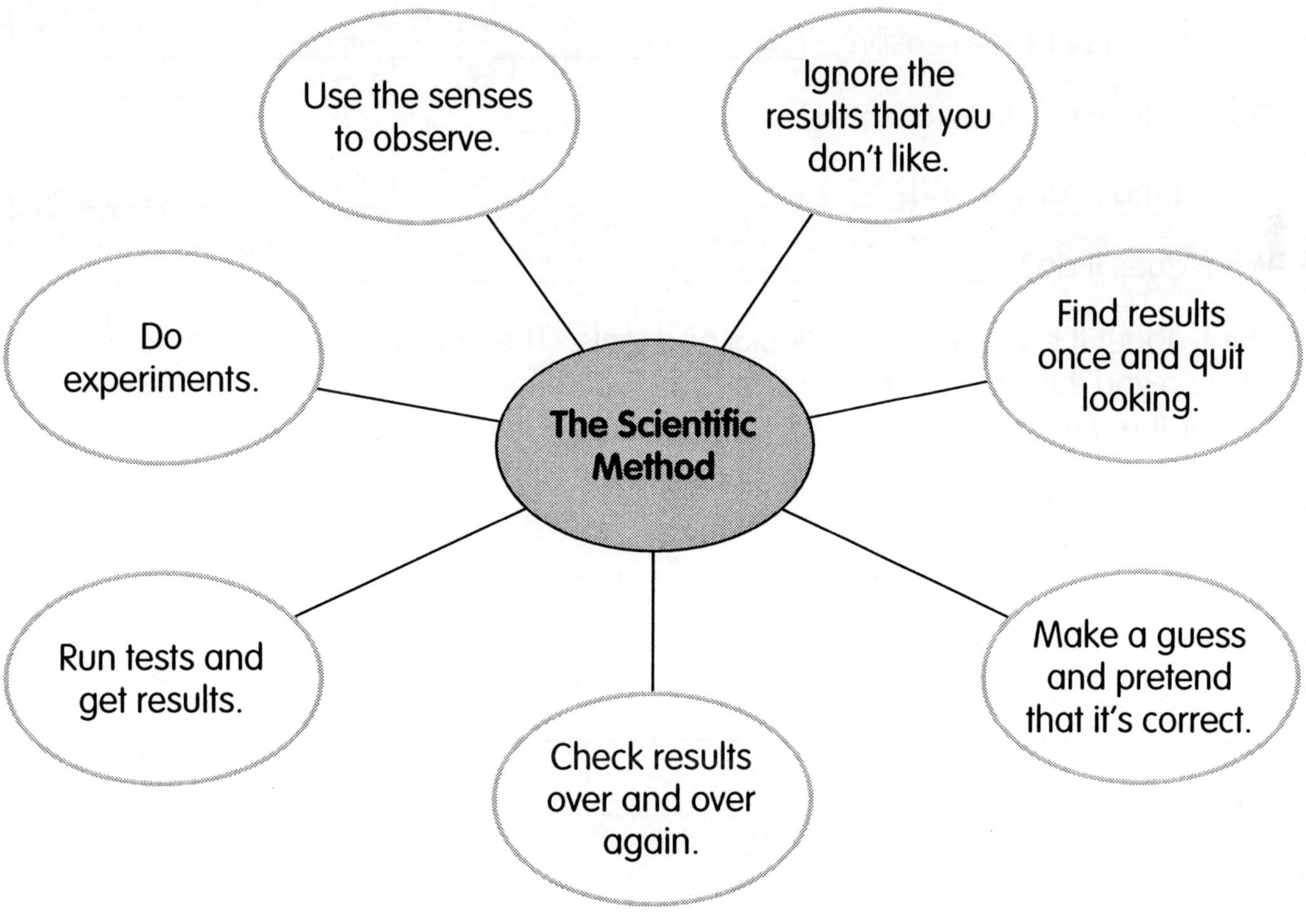

Warm-Up 102

Making Some Observations

Name: ______________________________

Scientists are great learners. They have to be! In order for scientists to learn how things work and find solutions to problems, they have to learn everything they can. They have to ask themselves questions and find reasons for the answers.

Directions: Practice being a scientist. Find an object nearby. It can be a pencil, an eraser, your desk, or the bottle your water comes in. Study that one object very closely. Take a few minutes to learn everything you can about it. Use your discoveries to fill in the lines below.

Name of the Object ______________________________

What is its shape? ______________________________

What is its color? ______________________________

What is it made out of? ______________________________

Does it feel hard or soft? ______________________________

Does it bend or move easily? ______________________________

Does it have any taste or smell? ______________________________

Does it make any sound? ______________________________

What does it do? ______________________________

Think about the way the object looks and feels. Then think about what it does. Why do you think an object that does that would look and feel that way? Give two or three reasons.

____

____

____

____

____

A Light That Keeps Glowing

Warm-Up 103

Name: ______________________________

People used to burn oil to make light. This light didn't last long, and the oil was dangerous. It was too easy to start a fire by tipping a lamp over.

Many inventors worked on creating an electric light. One of the most famous to do this was Thomas Edison. People say that he invented the light bulb, but he was not the only one who worked on this invention.

Edison and others tried to put many different materials in their light bulbs. Most of these materials didn't work. They burned out too quickly. Finally, a good material was found. This material was able to stay lit for over 1,200 hours!

Directions: Look at the light bulb. It is filled with letters. Cross out every letter that is in the word **LIGHT**. Which letters are left? Write those letters in order to spell the name of the material that made electric light possible.

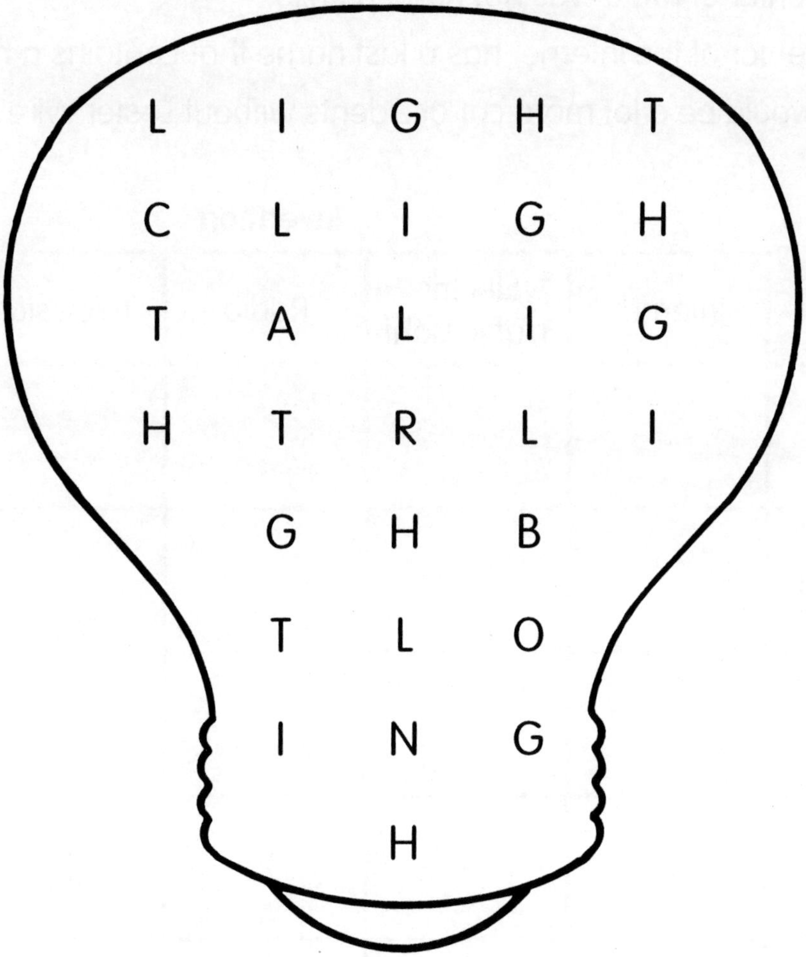

Write the name of the material here:

___ ___ ___ ___ ___ ___

Warm-Up 104

Who Invented What?

Name: ______________________________

There are some things we use almost every day. We may even take some of these things for granted. But a person (and often a lot of people) had to invent these things. And once these things were invented, a lot of improvements were needed to make them into the products we use today.

Directions: Use the clues to match each person's name with the product he invented or improved. Use the chart below to keep track of who did what. Each name on the left matches an invention on the top. Using the clues, put a checkmark in each box that matches the person to the correct product. The clues might also help you eliminate certain people from certain products. If so, then put an **X** in those boxes. The information from Clue #1 has already been recorded in the chart.

Clue #1: Charles Strite invented a machine that popped up toasted bread.

Clue #2: The inventor of radio was not named Philo.

Clue #3: The inventor of the Internet has a last name that contains a hyphen (dash).

Clue #4: There would be a lot more car accidents without Lester Wire's invention.

	Invention				
Inventor	Internet	Electric Traffic Light	Radio	Television	Pop-Up Toaster
Tim Berners-Lee					
Philo Farnsworth					
Guglielmo Marconi					
Charles Strite	X	X	X	X	✓
Lester Wire					

Unit 12 — Life Science: Scientists & Inventors

Warm-Up 105

Failures That Became Successes

Name: ______________________________

Not all great inventions were planned. In fact, some things we use all the time started out as failures.

A sticky note is a piece of paper that you can write on and put just about anywhere. It is just the right amount of sticky. You can move it, and the paper won't tear. Well, the glue that makes sticky notes so useful was not what the inventor meant to make. His name was Spencer Silver. He was trying to make a really strong glue. Instead, it was very weak. Still, he thought his new glue could be useful. No one would listen. Years later, a man named Arthur Fry believed in Silver's invention. Together, Fry and Silver made sticky notes.

Who doesn't like chocolate chip cookies? They were another mistake. A baker named Ruth Wakefield ran out of baker's chocolate. She tried using a different type of chocolate, but it didn't melt into the cookie. The chunks just got soft. She tasted her mistake and realized it was delicious!

Then there's the story of a Scottish scientist named Alexander Fleming. One day, he forgot to put a lid on one of his lab dishes. Something in the air landed in just the right place on the dish. Fleming noticed later that there were no bacteria in that spot. This led to the discovery of penicillin. Penicillin is a medicine that has saved millions of lives. It is still used today.

Directions: The facts about the three inventions are written below. For each one, there is one "fact" that is not true. Find it and cross it out.

---

1. Glue for Sticky Notes

invented by Spencer Silver

didn't tear paper when removed

became successful right away

---

2. Chocolate Chip Cookies

invented by Ruth Fry

used the wrong kind of chocolate

new cookie tasted great

---

3. Penicillin

discovered by an American scientist

found after a lid wasn't closed

is still used today as medicine

Warm-Up 106

Word Study

Name: ______________________________

There are many different types of scientist. Some scientists study animals, some study plants, and some study rocks. Some scientists use microscopes to study tiny things. Other scientists use telescopes to study huge planets and stars. Each type of scientist has a different name.

Directions: It's time to match the name of a scientist with what he or she does. Use the alphabet key to fill in the letters of each scientist's name. The first one has been done for you.

Alphabet Key

a	b	c	d	e	f	g	h	i	j	k	l	m
1	2	3	4	5	6	7	8	9	10	11	12	13

n	o	p	q	r	s	t	u	v	w	x	y	z
14	15	16	17	18	19	20	21	22	23	24	25	26

	Name of the Scientist	What He or She Studies
1.	b o t a n i s t 2 15 20 1 14 9 19 20	plants
2.	__ __ __ __ __ __ __ __ __ 26 15 15 12 15 7 9 19 20	animals
3.	__ __ __ __ __ __ __ __ __ 7 5 15 12 15 7 9 19 20	Earth and its history
4.	__ __ __ __ __ __ __ __ __ 16 8 25 19 9 3 9 19 20	matter and energy
5.	__ __ __ __ __ __ __ __ 12 9 14 7 21 9 19 20	human language
6.	__ __ __ __ __ __ __ __ __ __ 3 25 20 15 12 15 7 9 19 20	cells

What's the Matter?

Warm-Up 107

Name: ______________________________

Everything on Earth is made up of matter. The tiniest parts that make up that matter are called atoms. They are far too small to see. These tiny atoms combine to make molecules, which are also too small to see. But molecules combine to make up everything we see around us.

Most combinations of molecules form into one of three states of matter: solid, liquid, or gas. A rock is a solid. Water is a liquid. Air is a gas. Why are some things solid and other things liquid or a gas?

If molecules are very close together, they make a solid. Things that are solid have their own shape. That is because their molecules do not move around easily.

They bond (stick together) strongly. They stay where they are, so the thing that they make can keep its shape.

In a liquid, the molecules are not so close together. Liquids do not have their own shape. The molecules move around too easily. The molecules in a liquid do not bond as strongly as the ones that are part of a solid. When you pour a liquid into a solid, like a glass, the liquid takes on the solid's shape—until you pour it out!

Molecules in a gas barely bond at all. They move around even more easily than the molecules of a liquid. There is more space between the molecules than there is between molecules of a liquid. This means that gases don't have their own shape? Their molecules don't bond very strongly. They spread out so far that usually you cannot see a gas at all.

What Did You Learn ?

1. Which state of matter can best keep its shape?

Ⓐ solid Ⓑ liquid Ⓒ gas

2. In which state of matter are the molecules the farthest apart?

Ⓐ solid Ⓑ liquid Ⓒ gas

3. Which of these things is most likely to **bond** to something?

Ⓐ a glass covered in oil Ⓑ a glass covered in glue Ⓒ a glass with nothing on it

4. Water is a liquid. If you freeze it, it turns into ice. Ice has it's own shape. Why is that? (**Hint:** Is ice a liquid?)

____

Warm-Up 108

States of Matter

Name: ______________________________________

On Earth, most matter comes in three states: solid, liquid, and gas. Water is one common thing that we can see in all three states. Think about it:

Water

in liquid form *in solid form* *in gas form*

Can you think of other things that are solid? How about things that are liquid? What is a gas? (Be careful: The type of "gas" we put in our car is in liquid form!)

Directions: Draw an example of each type of matter. You can draw anything other than the water examples that were drawn for you.

Liquid

Solid

Gas

As a Matter of Fact

Name: ________________________________

On Earth, there are three main states of matter: solid, liquid, and gas.

Directions: Look at each picture. Decide whether the arrow is pointing to a solid, a liquid, or a gas. Circle the correct word.

1.

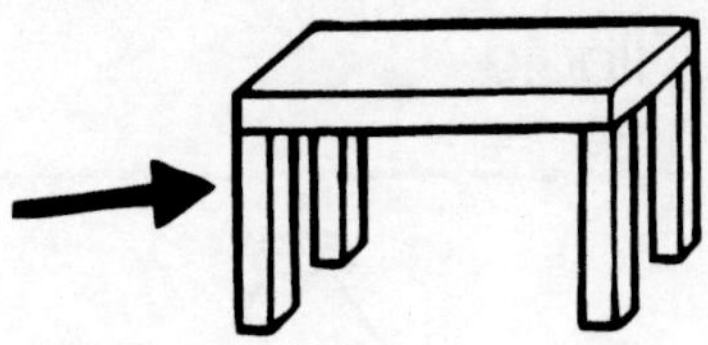

solid liquid gas

2.

solid liquid gas

3.

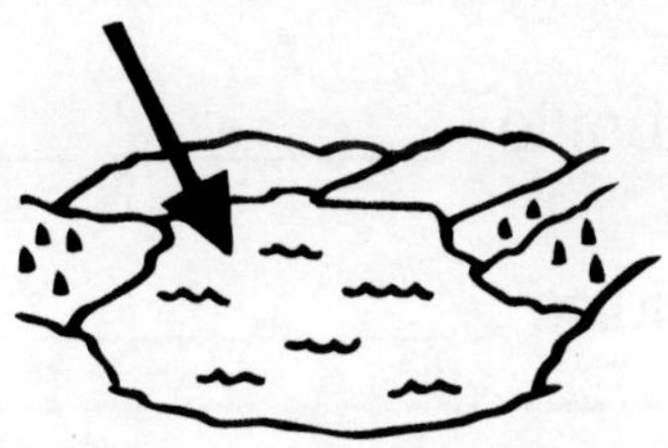

solid liquid gas

4.

solid liquid gas

5.

solid liquid gas

6.

solid liquid gas

7.

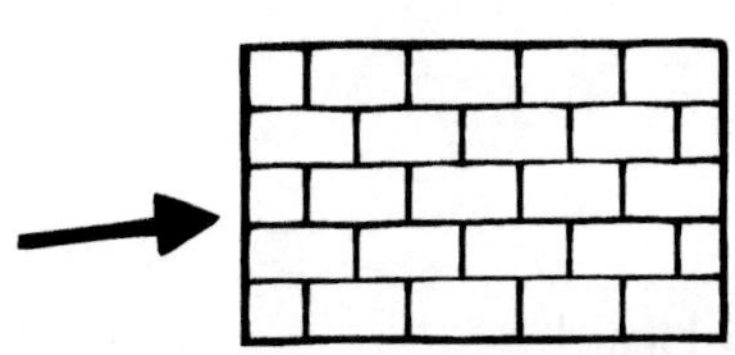

solid liquid gas

8.

solid liquid gas

Warm-Up 110

Liquids and Solids

Name: ______________________________

Liquids do not have any shape of their own. Think about some liquids that you know. Think about water or milk or juice. Do they have a shape? Or do they need to be put in a container to keep them from spilling all over the place? That container is not a liquid. It is a solid. It has shape.

Directions: Look at each picture. It shows a solid and a liquid. Write **solid** on the line next to each solid. Write **liquid** on the line next to each liquid.

1.

the milk ____________________

the carton ____________________

2.

the bottle ____________________

the juice ____________________

3.

the cup ____________________

the water ____________________

4.

the oil ____________________

the can ____________________

5.

the bowl ____________________

the water ____________________

the fish ____________________

Getting Back in Shape

Warm-Up 111

Name: ______________________________

Many things will change their shape and their state of matter when they are heated up or cooled down. Some of those things can never go back to the shape they used to be. Others can.

Directions: For each question, look at the first object. Then, look at what has happened to it after it has been changed. Think carefully. Can the object ever go back to the state it was in for the first picture? Write **yes** or **no** in the "Can It Go Back?" column.

	Object	How It Changed	What It Became	Can It Go Back?
1.	 **water**	frozen		
2.	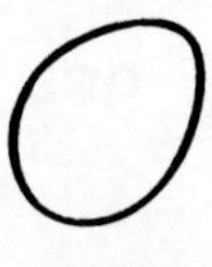 **egg**	heated up	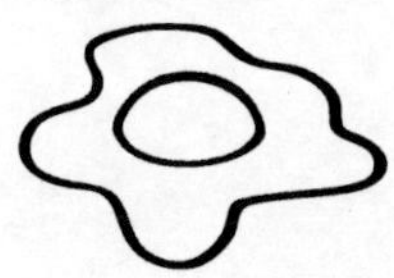	
3.	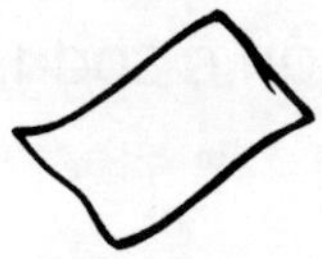 **paper**	heated up	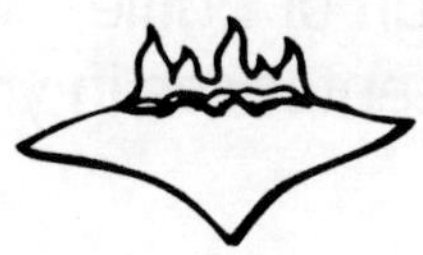	
4.	 **vegetables**	frozen		
5.	 **leaf**	heated up		

Warm-Up 112

All Shook Up and Nowhere to Go

Name: ______________________________

Have you ever shaken a soda can and then opened it? If you have, then you know what happens. Soda explodes everywhere! Why does that happen?

Soda contains a gas called carbon dioxide. In your unopened soda can or bottle, the carbon dioxide is in liquid form. Your soda can or bottle keeps the carbon dioxide this way. It does that with pressure. There is a lot of pressure inside a soda can or bottle.

When you open a soda can, the pressure is released. This allows the carbon dioxide to escape. It escapes as a gas. This makes those fizzy bubbles!

When you shake the can, a lot of bubbles get stuck to the sides of the can. They are under a lot of pressure, but they can't escape. Instead, the liquid soda flies out of the can when you open it. Then, everybody gets wet and sticky!

Directions: Answer these questions.

1. There are three states of matter: solid, liquid, and gas. Which state of matter never escapes from the soda can? Circle your answer.

   solid   **liquid**   **gas**

2. Cans or bottles with juice in them often say "Shake Well." Why do you think it's okay to shake a juice can or bottle? What makes it different than a soda can or bottle? Use complete sentences in your answer.

Warm-Up 113

Name: ______________________________________

Everything you can see on Earth is made up of smaller parts called molecules. Words are also made up of smaller parts called letters. Some words even have smaller words in them.

Directions: Look at each bigger word below. Each names an object that is a solid, liquid, or gas. Find the smaller word hidden inside. Use the clue to help you. The first one has been done for you.

Note: If you need extra help, use the **Word Box** below.

Bigger Word	Clue	Answer
1. pa<u>per</u>	type of animal	a p e
2. carbon	something you drive	___ ___ ___
3. oxygen	type of animal	___ ___
4. steam	type of drink	___ ___ ___
5. honey	small number	___ ___ ___
6. juice	frozen water	___ ___ ___
7. chair	what you breathe	___ ___ ___
8. vegetable	where you sit to eat	___ ___ ___ ___ ___
9. street	type of tall plant	___ ___ ___ ___

Word Box

air	ice	table
~~ape~~	one	tea
car	ox	tree

Warm-Up 114

Everything Is in Motion

Name: ______________________________

You are always moving. Everything in the universe is. Earth is moving around the sun, and the sun is moving around in space. Some things are moving so slowly that you don't even feel them moving.

This movement never stops. It is called motion. Motion doesn't stop, but it can change. Objects in motion can speed up or slow down or change direction. What makes them speed up or slow down or change direction? Forces do.

Some forces are easy to see. If you hit a ball with a bat, the ball goes in a different direction. You have used force to change the way the ball moves. Other forces cannot be seen. Gravity is a force that cannot be seen. Gravity pulls objects toward Earth. A ball that is thrown up into the air, for example, always falls back down to the ground. Gravity is the force that pulls the ball down to the ground. If there were no gravity on Earth, the ball might keep floating up and away.

What Did You Learn ?

1. Which thing is always moving?

Ⓐ Earth
Ⓑ the sun
Ⓒ you
Ⓓ All answers are correct.

2. A bat hitting a ball and changing its direction is an example of

Ⓐ force.
Ⓑ gravity.
Ⓒ direction.
Ⓓ pull.

3. What can't objects in motion do?

Ⓐ go faster
Ⓑ go slower
Ⓒ change direction
Ⓓ stop completely

Challenge: Now look at this statement. Circle **True** or **False**. Give a reason for your answer. Take your best guess.

You are not in motion when you are sitting still in a moving car. **True** **False**

____

____

____

____

What's Truly on the Move?

Name: ______________________________

We often use the words *motion* and *speed* to talk about how objects move.

- An object is in motion if it is changing positions (moving).
- Speed is the measure of an object's rate of motion. Speed is usually measured by the time it takes for an object to travel a certain distance. If an object moves faster, its speed increases (becomes greater). If the object slows down, its speed decreases (becomes less).

Directions: Look at these cars. They are in motion. Behind each is a statement about motion or speed. If the statement is true, color the car. If the statement is false, draw an **X** through the car.

1. An object is in motion if it changes position.

2. The word *increases* means "to become less."

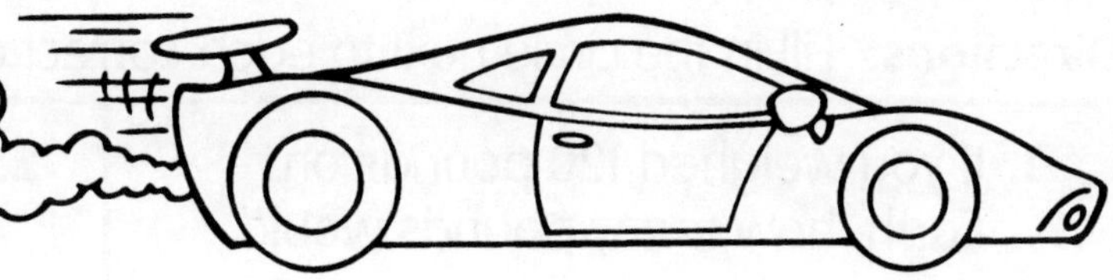

3. When an object moves, its speed can never increase.

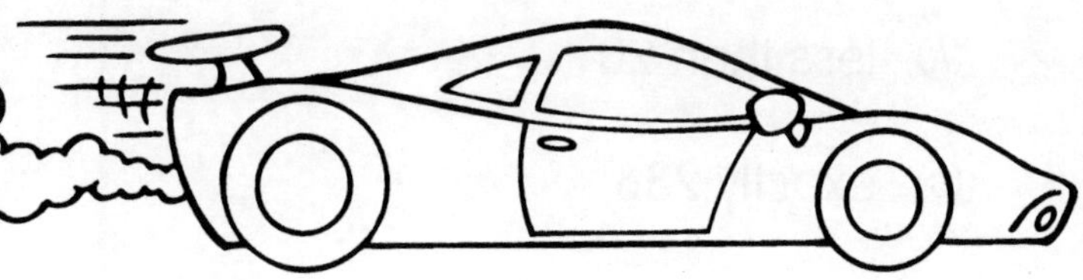

4. We measure time and distance to find speed.

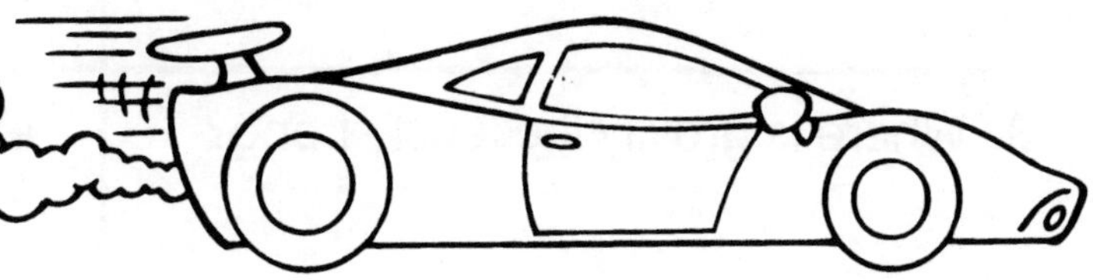

5. Speed is how fast an object is moving.

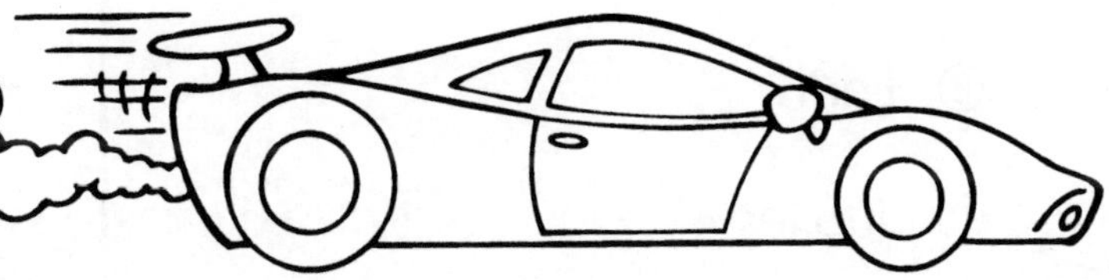

Warm-Up 116

What Goes Up Must Come Down

Name: ______________________________

What happens if you throw a ball up in the air? It falls down to the ground, right? This is because of a force called *gravity*. Gravity pulls things down to the ground. It holds them there, too.

You can't see gravity, but it is always on Earth. Its pull is strong. Earth is a big planet with a lot of mass. Mass is how much matter something is made of. Objects that have more mass also create more gravity.

The moon is very big, but it does not have nearly as much mass as Earth. So the moon's gravity is not as strong as Earth's. You could bounce around and jump high on the moon. You would weigh less there. If you weigh 100 pounds on Earth, you would weigh about 17 pounds on the moon. You would still have the same amount of mass inside you. You would just weigh less because there is less gravity to weigh you down.

On the other hand, Jupiter has a lot more mass than Earth. Jupiter has the most mass of any planet in our solar system. The pull of gravity on Jupiter is very strong. It would be much harder to move on Jupiter. A 100-pound person would weigh about 236 pounds on Jupiter.

Directions: Fill in the circle next to each correct answer.

1. If you weighed 120 pounds on Earth, how many pounds would you weigh on Jupiter?

Ⓐ less than 20

Ⓑ exactly 236

Ⓒ more than 236

2. Which of these places has the most mass?

Ⓐ the moon

Ⓑ Earth

Ⓒ Jupiter

3. Where is gravity the least strong?

Ⓐ the moon

Ⓑ Earth

Ⓒ Jupiter

4. *Mass* means the same thing as *weight*.

Ⓐ true

Ⓑ false

Ⓒ only on the moon

Red Light, Green Light

Name: ______________________________

Cars are in motion as they drive down the street. What happens when a car comes to a traffic light?

If the light is green, the car can keep going. The driver pushes the gas pedal. Gas and oil move through the car and keep its engine moving.

If the light is red, the car must stop. The driver pushes the brake pedal. Brakes use friction to slow the car down. Friction happens when two materials rub against each other. Friction causes an object in motion to slow down. The oil and the gas in cars make the friction less. This allows the car to move smoothly.

Directions: Read each example of friction.

- Color the **red light** if the example describes an event with a lot of friction. Remember, friction slows things down.
- Color the **green light** if the example describes an event with not very much friction. When there is little friction, objects can move faster and more smoothly.

1. a hocky puck sliding across ice RED GREEN	**2.** a square block rolling through a bush RED GREEN
3. a toy car rolling into a brick wall RED GREEN	**4.** a toy car rolling down a smooth ramp RED GREEN

Warm-Up 118

The Science of Making Waves

Name: ______________________________

Have you been to the beach and watched waves rolling in toward the shore? What makes those waves? Why do they rise and fall like they do? There are many forces that cause waves to look and act the way that they do.

Wind is one force that makes waves. Wind blows across the surface of the ocean. The wind tries to drag the surface of the water with it. The water pressure below the surface pushes the water up, too. What makes the water come back down? Gravity does. Gravity is a force that pulls things back toward Earth.

As the wave gets closer to the shore, friction also helps make waves. Friction is a force that slows down motion. The friction of the water rubbing against the sand slows the water down near the bottom. The water near the top is not slowed down as much. It keeps going fast. It rises up. Then, gravity starts to pull it down. The top of the wave curls and falls back down to the ground. Have you ever had a wave fall right on top of you?

Directions: Look at each picture. Read each question. Circle your answer.

---

1. The surface of the water is being pulled up. Which force is causing this?

friction **gravity** **wind**

---

2. The bottom of the water is slowing down as it gets close to shore. Which force is causing this?

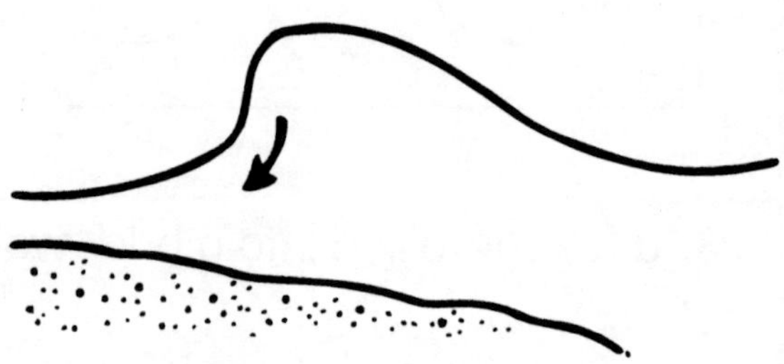

friction **gravity** **wind**

---

3. The top of the water is curling and falling back to Earth. Which force is causing this?

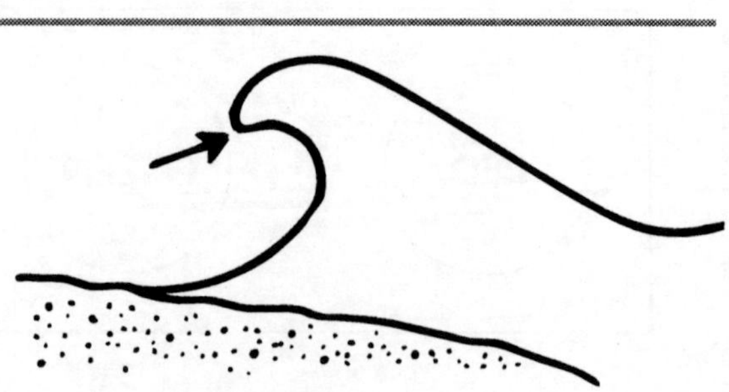

friction **gravity** **wind**

The Push and Pull of Force

Warm-Up 119

Name: ____________________________________

Everything you see is in motion in some way. Forces make things move. Two simple types of force are pushing and pulling. You push and pull things all of the time.

- A **push** moves things away from you.
- A **pull** moves things toward you.

Directions: Look at each picture and description. Does it show a push or a pull? Circle the correct answer.

1. picking a flower  **push** **pull**	**2.** moving a cart  **push** **pull**	**3.** kicking a ball 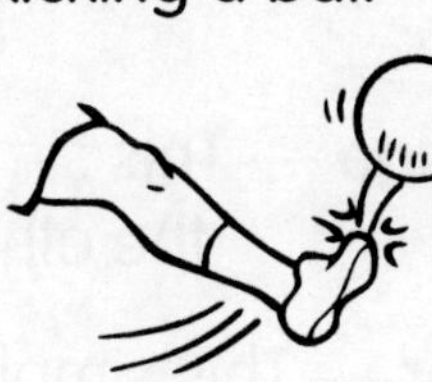 **push** **pull**
4. opening a door 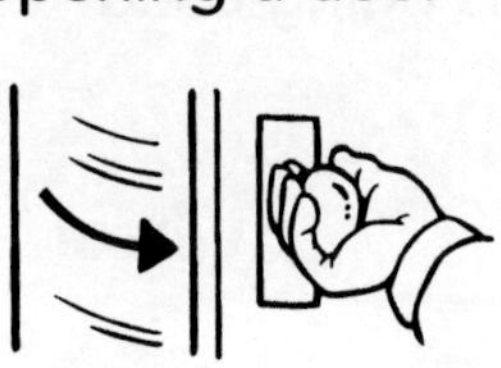 **push** **pull**	**5.** climbing a rope  **push** **pull**	**6.** painting a picture 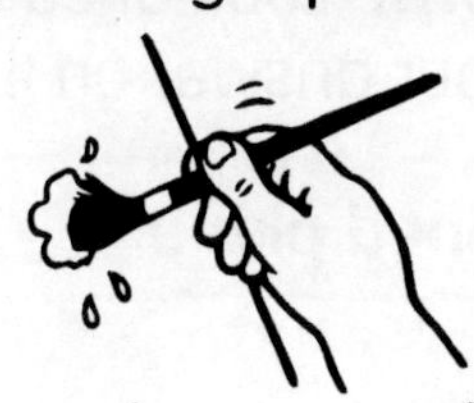 **push** **pull**

Now draw yourself pushing or pulling something.

Warm-Up 120

The Most Simple of Machines

Name: ______________________________

Machines help us get things done. When you hear the word *machine*, you might think of a car or a computer. Not all machines have engines or need electricity, though. Not all machines have many parts. Some machines are very simple. In fact, some are called "simple machines."

Here are descriptions of some simple machines:

- **wheel** — A wheel by itself is a simple machine. It can help you move things that are heavy.
- **inclined plane** — A ramp is an example of this kind of simple machine. It helps you get things from one place to another.
- **wedge** — This simple machine is thick on one end and much thinner on the other. It can help you pry things apart.
- **lever** — This simple machine is a sturdy beam or rod. One end stays put, while the other end pushes or moves things.

Directions: Look at each picture. What kind of simple machine is being used? Write your answer on the line.

inclined plane	lever	wedge	wheel

1.

____

2.

____

3.

____

4.

____

Name: ____________________

When things move, they are in *motion*. Words that show motion or action are called *verbs*. Look at this sentence:

We walk to the park on Sundays, and we fly our kites there.

In that sentence, there are two verbs. The word *walk* tells us how this person got to the park. The word *fly* tells us what they did with their kites while they were at the park. Both words show motion. They show action.

Directions: Read the story in the box. Underline every word that shows motion or action. Rewrite each word on the lines below the story.

> My team played baseball last night. Craig hit two home runs, and Bobby stole three bases. Jim pitched a lot of strikes. I caught many balls in the outfield. My mom and dad cheered me on.

Rewrite the verbs here:

Now write a sentence of your own. Use at least one word that shows motion. Underline the word that shows motion.

Warm-Up 122

Our Lives Are Full of Energy

Name: ______________________________

What do light, sound, and heat have in common? They are all forms of energy. So is electricity. So is magnetism, which is the force that makes metal stick to magnets. Energy is all around us, even though we usually can't see it. Energy powers our computers, lights up our houses, keeps us warm or cool, and helps us move. There is nothing that can be done without energy!

Much of the energy on Earth comes from the sun. For example, the sun provides energy to plants. We eat the plants (and we also eat animals who get their energy from plants). This gives us the energy we need to think and move and even sleep.

What Did You Learn ?

1. Look at the pictures. Circle every picture that shows energy being used.

2. In the box to the right, draw a picture of the thing from which Earth gets its energy.

Plugging in to Electricity

Warm-Up 123

Name: ______________________________

One form of energy that we use all of the time is electricity. Without electricity, we couldn't use our computers, TVs, or refrigerators. Electricity is what powers anything that plugs into a wall or uses batteries.

Electricity is usually in one of two states. It is either static or current. *Static electricity* does not move. *Current electricity* moves from one place to another. Static electricity is often caused when things rub together.

A good example of both kinds of electricity is lightning. Most lightning happens because rain clouds move across the sky. As they do this, they rub against the air. This rubbing builds up static electricity inside the rain cloud. Once too much static electricity has built up, the cloud releases it. A bolt of lightning shoots down from the cloud. It strikes the ground. The lightning is an example of current electricity. The electricity goes from the cloud to ground.

Directions: Look at the picture. What type of electricity is being used? Circle your answer. Then explain why you answered this way.

static **current**

____

____

____

____

____

____

____

____

Warm-Up 124

Have You Heard About This?

Name: ____________________________

Energy is all around us. A lot of it can't be seen. Some of it can be heard, though. After all, sound is energy! When something makes a sound, it moves the air. The air moves in waves that we cannot see. The air moves all the way to our ears.

We measure the loudness of things in *decibels*. The higher the number of decibels, the louder something is.

Directions: The graph shows how loud some things are. Use it to answer each question below. Fill in the circle next to each correct answer.

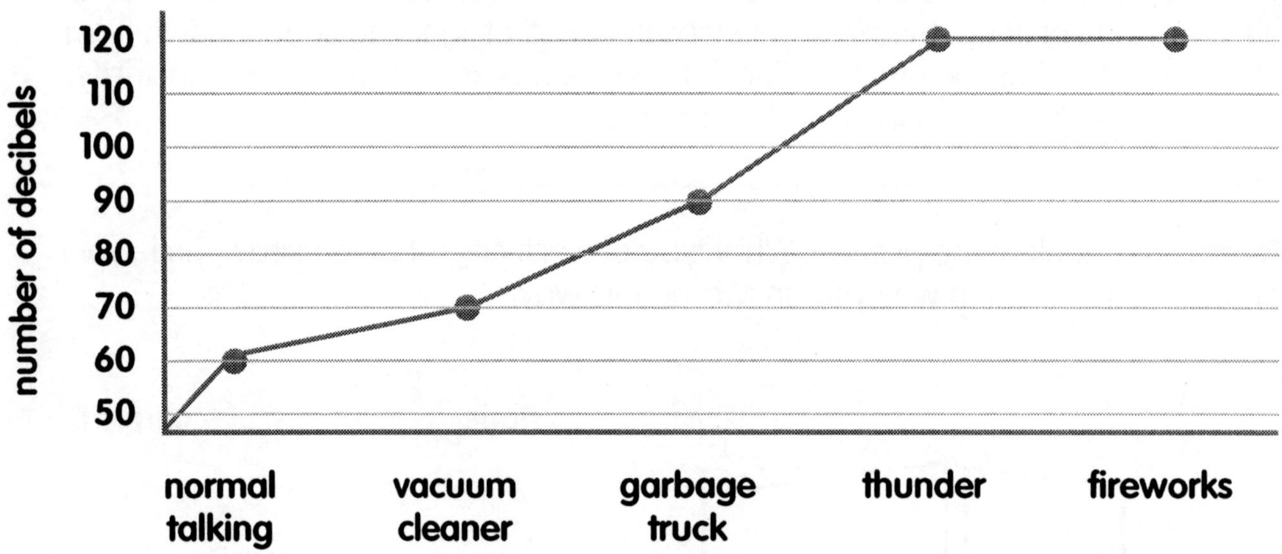

1. Which of these noises is loudest?

Ⓐ garbage truck   Ⓑ fireworks   Ⓒ vacuum cleaner

2. Which of these is *not* 120 decibels?

Ⓐ thunder   Ⓑ fireworks   Ⓒ garbage truck

3. If normal talking is about 60 decibels, which number might show the number of decibels in a whisper?

Ⓐ 20   Ⓑ 70   Ⓒ 100

4. Can you think of noises that are louder than thunder or fireworks? Write two noises that you think are louder.

____________________   ____________________

Lightning, Then Thunder

Name: ______________________________

We usually say the words "thunder and lightning" in that order. But maybe we should say "lightning" first. Think about a stormy night. It's dark and rainy. You see a bolt of lightning light up the sky. Then, seconds later, you hear the loud boom of thunder. The lightning and the thunder don't seem to happen at the same time.

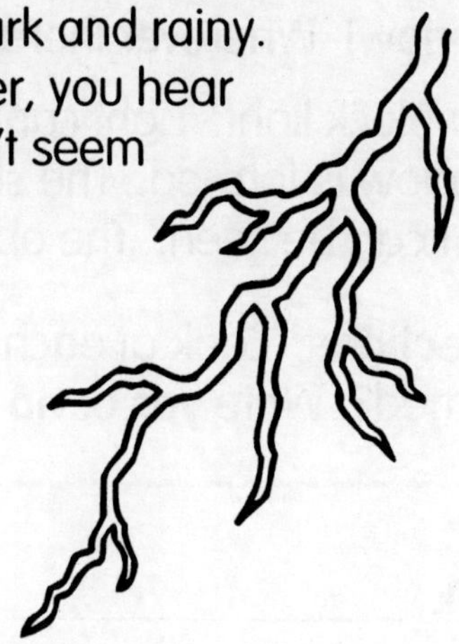

The lightning (light) and thunder (sound) *do* happen together. There's a reason, though, that we see the lightning before we hear the thunder. It is because light travels faster than sound. Light travels at about 186,000 miles per second! Sound "only" travels about 770 miles per hour. So the light gets to our eyes much more quickly than the sound gets to our ears.

Directions: Read Story #1 and Story #2. Then, answer the questions below.

Story #1

We watched a baseball game at the stadium today. Our seats were far from the field. The best part of the game was when my favorite player hit a home run. I heard the loud crack of his wooden bat hitting the ball. Then, I saw him swing his bat a second later. That ball must have traveled 500 feet through the air!

Story #2

I watched a movie being made today. I got to see a crash scene being filmed. I stood far back, where I would be safe. The director said, "Action!" Two fast cars smashed into each other. A big ball of fire went up into the sky. Then, I heard a huge explosion. It looked so real, but I was glad no one was hurt.

Which story could really happen? ______________________________

Explain your answer. ______________________________

____

____

____

Warm-Up 126

You and Your Shadow

Name: ______________________________

Who is always with you when you walk under the sun or any other bright light? It's your shadow! Wherever there is bright light and you, your shadow can't be far away.

You block light. Light cannot be seen through you. When an solid object blocks light, a shadow is formed. The shadow is dark. This is because the object blocks the light. No light can be seen. The object is always between the shining light and the dark shadow.

Directions: Look at each picture. Does it show the correct way that a shadow is formed? Write **yes** or **no** on the line.

1. ______________________

2. ______________________

3. ______________________

4. ______________________

The Color That Keeps You Cooler

Name: ____

The sun is the source of all energy on Earth. It sends light and heat to our planet. On some days, it feels as if the sun is sending extra light and extra heat. You probably want to wear a short-sleeved shirt on days like that. You want to keep as cool as possible. Did you know that the color of your shirt is important, too? It's true!

For example, black shirts and white shirts do much different things with the light from the sun. Shirts that are black take in almost all of the light. They don't reflect much of it at all. In a sense, the light and the heat that goes with it are soaked into the shirt. White shirts reflect almost all of the light and the heat from the sun. They don't take much of it in. The light and the heat bounce right off of the shirt. This is why a white shirt can help you stay cooler than a black shirt can.

Directions: Look at Sam and Alex. They are about to go to an all-day music concert. The concert is outdoors in the hot desert. Write a few sentences with Alex telling Sam why a different shirt and hat might be better to wear.

Warm-Up 128

Attracted or Not?

Name: ______________________________

Many things that have iron and other metals are attracted to magnets. Put a magnet over these things, and they will be pulled toward the magnet!

Directions:

- Color the things below that are attracted to the magnet.
- Cross out the things that are not attracted to the magnet.

Remember, many metal things are attracted to magnets. Things that are made of glass, plastic, or wood are not attracted to magnets.

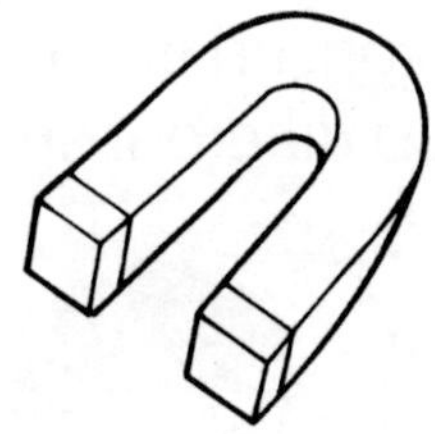
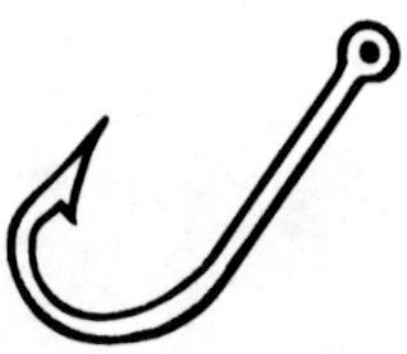

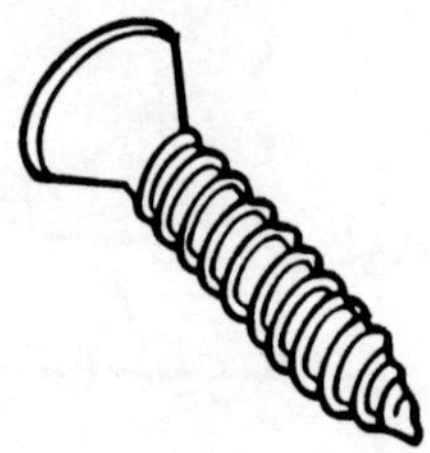

Name: ______________________________

The sun is the source of all energy on Earth.

Directions: Draw lines to match the clues to each energy word. The first one is done for you. Then, fill in the puzzle below.

Energy Clues	Energy Words
1. This is the kind of energy we can hear.	plants
2. We get energy from the sun by eating these.	heat
3. We even use energy while we do this.	sound
4. We burn this type of fuel for energy.	sleep
5. This uses energy to attract metal objects.	magnet
6. We need this type of energy to keep us warm.	fossil

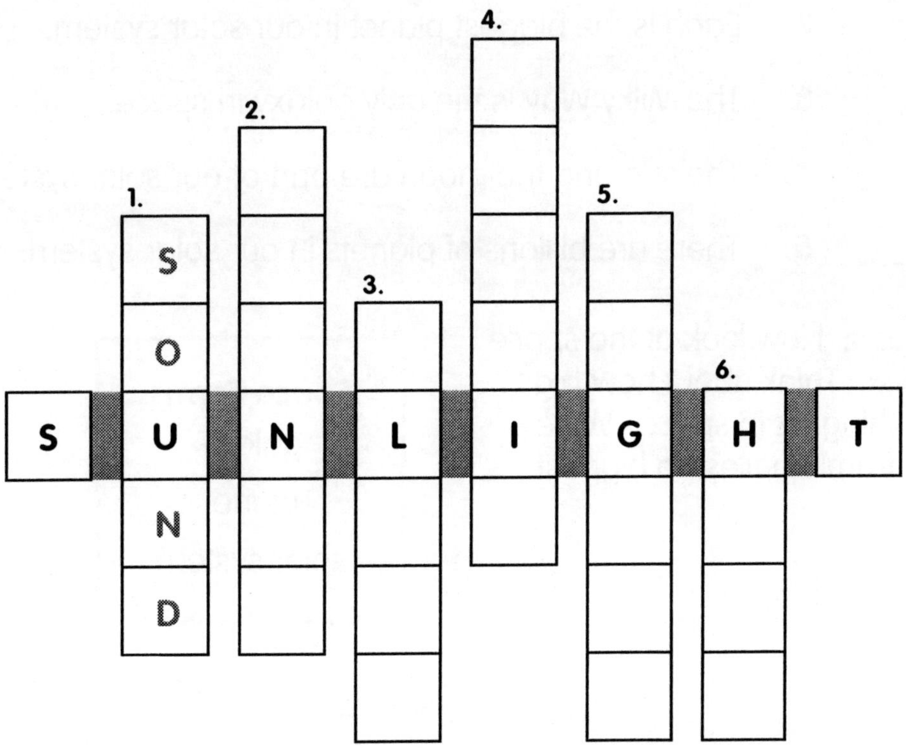

Warm-Up 130

Space, and Everything in It

Name: ________________________________

Space is huge. It contains our planet, which is called Earth. It is also where the sun, the moon, and the stars we see in the sky are. But that's only just a tiny bit of what is in space.

Think of how big our planet is. Earth is just one small part of a solar system. There are eight planets in our solar system, and Earth isn't even close to being the biggest.

Our solar system isn't the only solar system in space. It is one of many in our galaxy, which is called the Milky Way. There are billions of stars and billions of planets in the Milky Way. And the Milky Way is only one galaxy. There are billions of galaxies in space!

What Did You Learn ?

Part 1 Directions: Write **True** or **False** next to each sentence.

________________ **1.** Earth is part of a galaxy called the Milky Way.

________________ **2.** Earth is the biggest planet in our solar system.

________________ **3.** The Milky Way is the only galaxy in space.

________________ **4.** The sun and the moon are part of our solar system.

________________ **5.** There are billions of planets in our solar system.

Part 2 Directions: Now look at the space terms in the box. Think about how big each of these things is in space. Write them in order from smallest to biggest.

Space Terms
galaxy
planet
solar system

________________ **big** ________________ **bigger** ________________ **biggest**

The Sun and the Planets

Warm-Up 131

Name: ________________________________

There are eight planets in our solar system. These eight planets all go around the sun. Some are close to the sun. Some are very far from the sun. The planets that are closer to the sun are hotter. The planets that are farther from the sun are colder.

This diagram shows the sun and the eight planets in order:

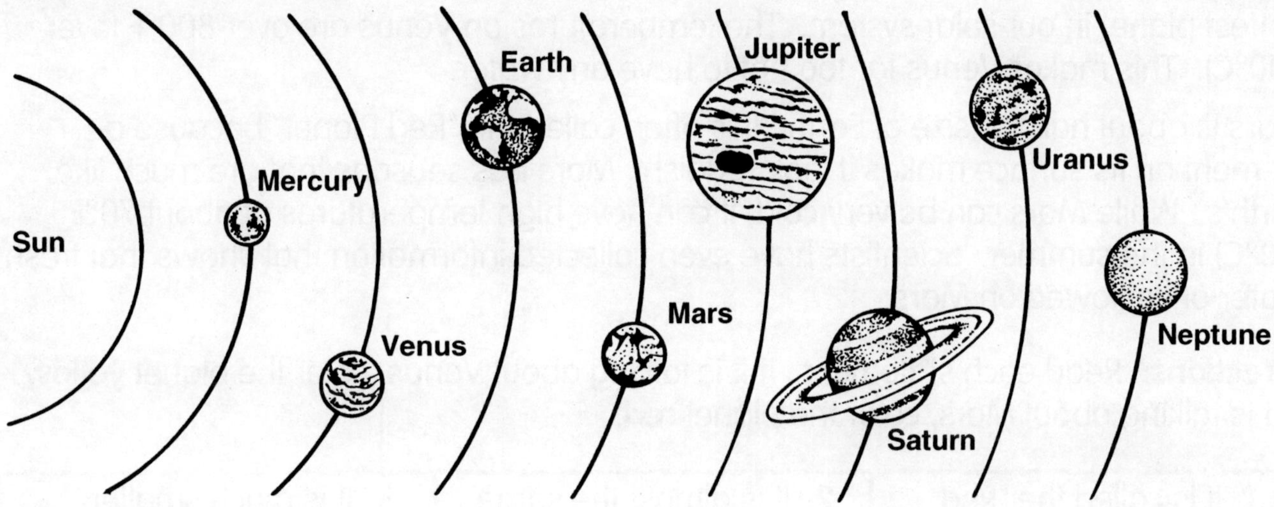

Directions: Use the diagram above to answer these questions. Fill in the circle of each correct answer.

1. Mercury is the 1st planet from the sun. Earth is the ________ planet from the sun.

Ⓐ 2nd Ⓑ 3rd Ⓒ 4th

2. ______________ is the planet farthest from the sun.

Ⓐ Mercury Ⓑ Saturn Ⓒ Neptune

3. Which one of these planets would most likely be coldest?

Ⓐ Uranus Ⓑ Venus Ⓒ Mars

What Am I ?

I am the largest planet in our solar system. I am the fifth planet from the sun.

I am _____ _____ _____ _____ _____ _____ _____.

Unit 16 — Earth & Space Science: Space

Warm-Up 132

Earth's Next-Door Neighbors

Name: ______________________________

Earth is the third planet from the sun. Venus is the second, and Mars is the fourth. In our solar system, Venus and Mars are our Earth's neighbors. However, they are very different planets.

Of all the planets, Venus is the closest to Earth. It is almost the same size as Earth. No other planet is so close to being the same size as Earth. But Venus is very hot. It is the hottest planet in our solar system. The temperatures on Venus are over 800°F (over 400°C). This makes Venus far too hot to have any water.

Mars is about half the size of Earth. It is often called the "Red Planet" because an element on its surface makes it look reddish. Mars has seasons that are much like Earth's. While Mars can be very cold, it can have high temperatures of about 70°F (20°C) in the summer. Scientists have even collected information that shows that fresh water once flowed on Mars.

Directions: Read each statement. If it is talking about Venus, color the planet **yellow**. If it is talking about Mars, color the planet **red**.

1. It is called the "Red Planet." 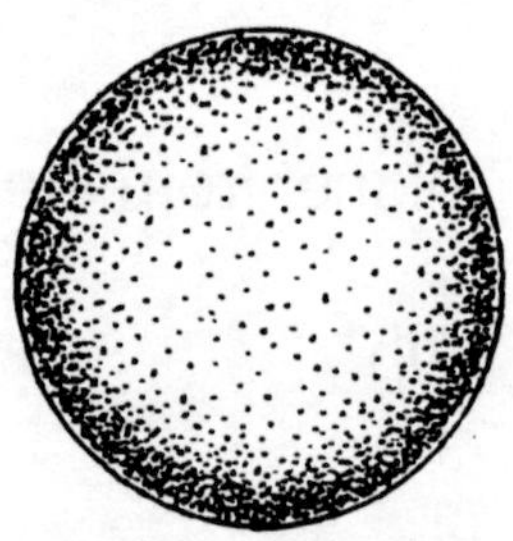	**2.** It is almost the same size as Earth. 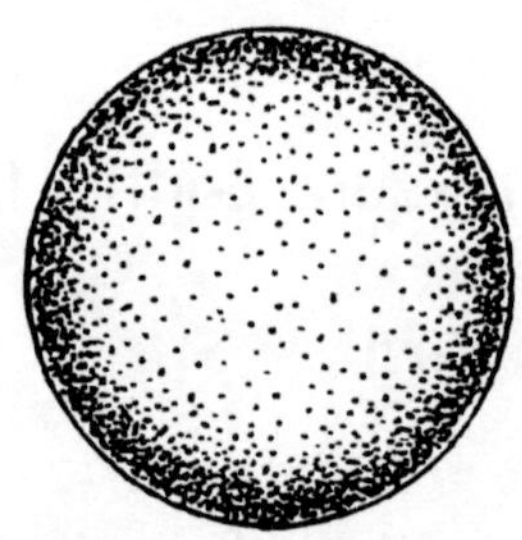	**3.** It is much smaller than Earth. 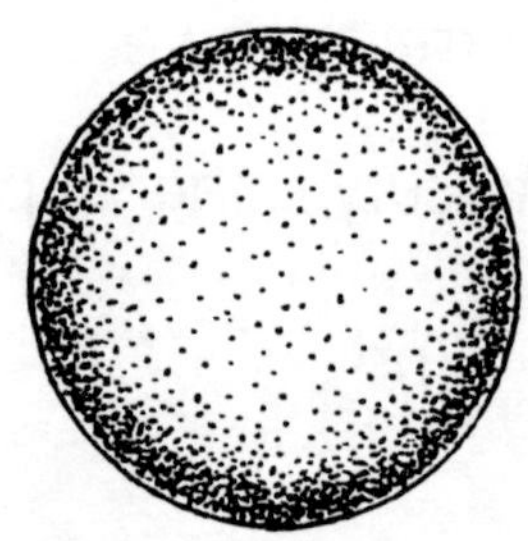
4. It is the second planet from the sun. 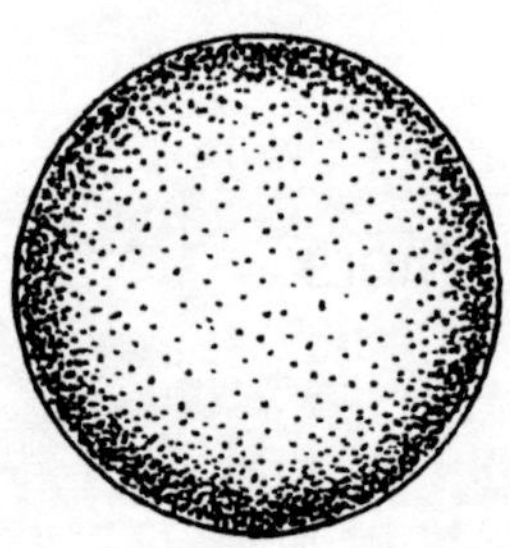	**5.** It has very hot temperatures. 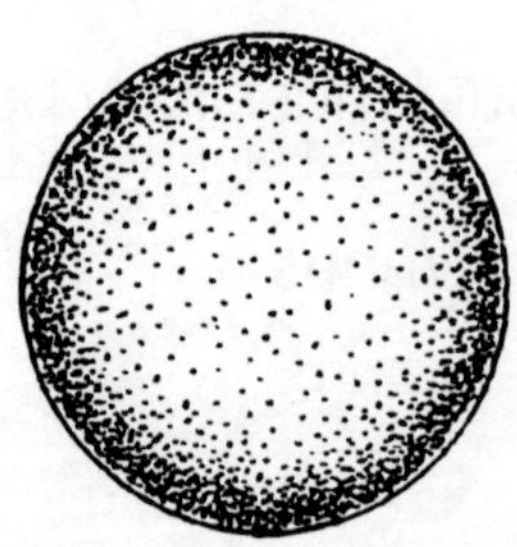	**6.** It has seasons like Earth does. 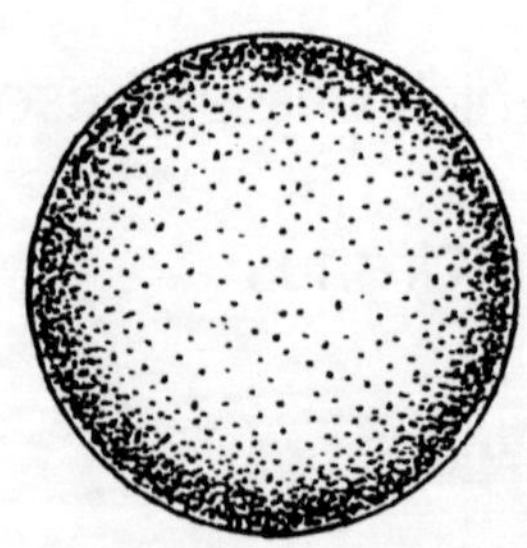

Extra: Which planet seems like it would be better to live on, Venus or Mars? On the back of this paper, write your choice and explain why you chose it.

Many, Many Moons

Name: ____

A moon is a natural object that orbits (goes around) a planet in space. Earth has one moon. Our moon always orbits around Earth. Some planets have no moons, while other planets have lots of moons. This chart shows how many moons each of the planets in our solar system has:

Mercury	Venus	Earth	Mars	Jupiter	Saturn	Uranus	Neptune
0	0	1	2	67	62	27	14

These numbers sometimes change. Scientists are always learning more about space. Sometimes they discover new moons. So there might be even more moons out there in space!

Directions: Fill in the circle for each correct answer.

1. Which of these planets has the most moons?

Ⓐ Mars Ⓑ Neptune Ⓒ Uranus

2. How many more moons does Jupiter have than Saturn?

Ⓐ 2 Ⓑ 5 Ⓒ 7

3. How many moons does Neptune have? Color in that number of moons.

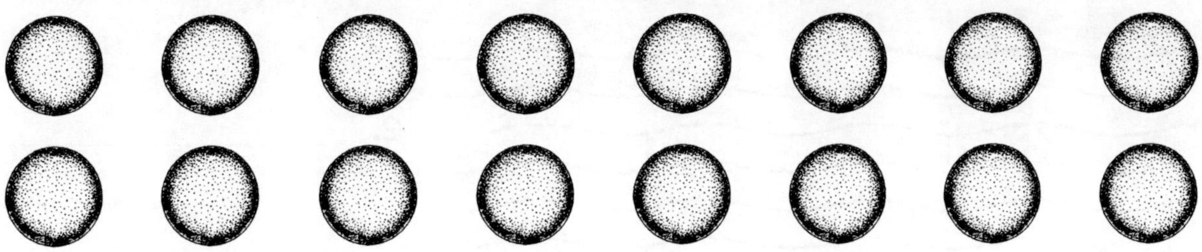

4. Look at the graph below. Which planet is Planet **Y**?

Ⓐ Mars Ⓑ Venus Ⓒ Earth

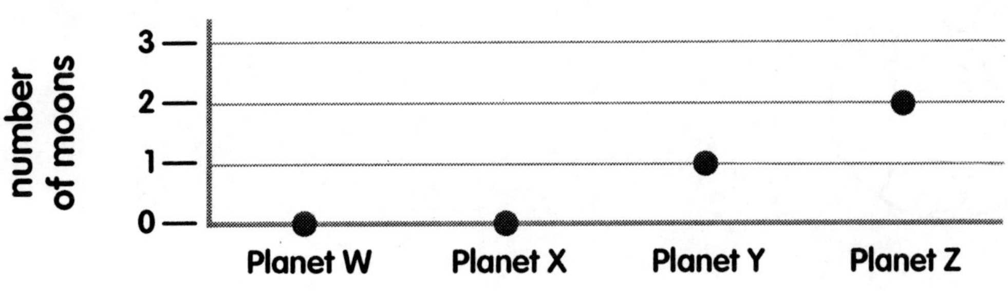

Warm-Up 134

Twinkle, Twinkle, Big Star

Name: ______________________________

The stars in the sky look small. They look like they twinkle. The truth is that the stars in the sky are very big, and they do not twinkle at all.

Stars are huge. They are bigger than Earth! They look small because they are so far away. We can only see them because they are so big and bright.

The light from stars has to travel far to get to Earth. There is a lot of stuff between us and those stars. There is a lot of air, for one thing. This air is always moving. We are looking at the stars through all of this moving air. It makes the stars look like they are twinkling. If you could get much closer to stars, you would see that they do not twinkle at all.

Directions: Look at the pictures. Write the name of each thing you see. Use the words in the box to help you.

air	**Earth**	**star**

1. ______________________

2. ______________________

3. ______________________

Stars with Hair?

Warm-Up 135

Name: ____________________________________

Comets are natural objects in space. They are like stars, but they look different. They have a thin, fuzzy tail of gas and ice on their ends. The word *comet* means "long-haired." They were named by a Greek philosopher named Aristotle. He thought comets looked like stars with hair.

Comets are made mostly of three things: ice, dust, and rocks. Scientists have seen over 4,000 different comets in space. But there are probably millions (or trillions) more. Not all comets can be seen from Earth.

One very famous comet is called Halley's Comet. When Halley's Comet comes by Earth, you can see it with just your eyes. For hundreds of years, people have watched Halley's Comet. They have noticed that it can be seen every 75 or 76 years. The last time it came close enough to Earth to be seen was in 1986. This means that Halley's Comet will be seen again in the year 2061. Be on the lookout for it!

Part 1 Directions: Look at the picture of the comet. Color its tail yellow. Then, write the names of the three ingredients that comets are made of.

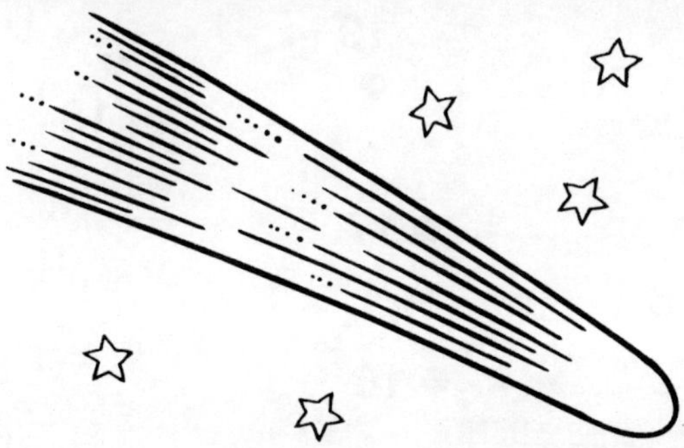

Ingredients

____

____

____

Part 2 Directions: How old will you be when Halley's Comet returns in 2061? ______

Do you think you'll want to see it? Tell why or why not.

____

____

____

____

____

____

Warm-Up 136

What Do You See in the Stars?

Name: ______________________________

Have you ever looked at a night sky that has lots of stars? Does it look like you could draw an object or an animal just by connecting the stars? People have been doing that for hundreds of years! They saw patterns in the stars. These patterns are called *constellations.*

One famous constellation is called Ursa Major. It is often called "Great Bear." One part of the Great Bear is said to look like a dipper. A dipper is a big, deep spoon that you might use to scoop up water. This part is called the Big Dipper. It is formed by seven bright stars.

Step 1: Use a **blue** crayon to connect the dots in order from **1** to **7**.

Step 2: Use a **blue** crayon to connect dot **4** to dot **7**.

Step 3: Use a **green** crayon to connect the dots in order from **7** to dot **20**.

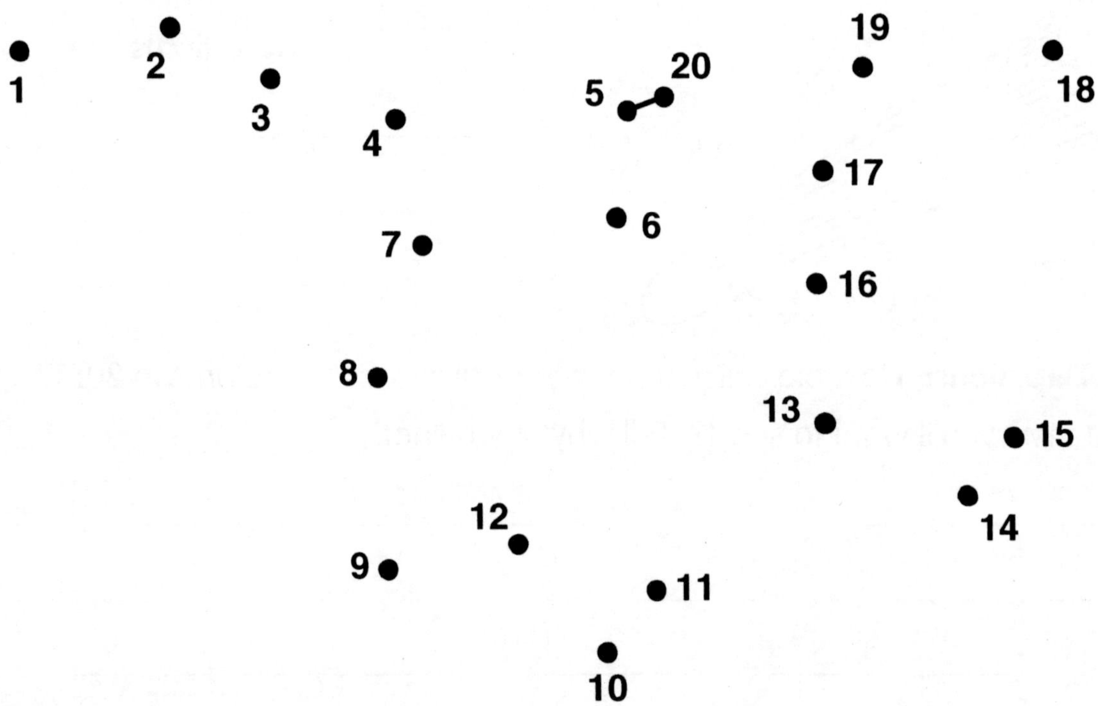

What Do You See?

1. What color is the Big Dipper in your drawing? **blue** **green**
2. Does the whole constellation look like a "Great Bear"? **yes** **no**
3. If you had to think of another name for this constellation, what would you call it? ______________________________

Warm-Up 137

Name: ________________________________

There are eight planets in our solar system. You might be asked to put them in the order they are from the sun. How can you learn and remember this order? Sometimes the best way to remember this kind of thing is to come up with a memory trick. Some people use the first letter of each planet's name to make a new sentence. This new sentence helps them remember the order.

Look at the first letter of each planet's name. Then, read the sentence below.

1	2	3	4	5	6	7	8
Mercury	Venus	Earth	Mars	Jupiter	Saturn	Uranus	Neptune
M	V	E	M	J	S	U	N
my	very	educated	mother	just	served	us	nachos.

Directions: Look at the five sentences below. Three of them could be used to help you remember the order of the planets. Two of them are not in the correct order. Write **Yes** on the line next to the ones that are correct. Write **No** on the line next to the ones that are not.

________ **1.** My very exciting motorboat joyfully sped up north.

________ **2.** Many vampires expertly make jellybeans every Sunday.

________ **3.** My valuable electric machine just saved us nothing.

________ **4.** More vegetables equals more juicy snacks you never eat.

________ **5.** Mike viewed expert magicians juggling some unsalted nuts.

Now can you come up with a sentence of your own to help you remember the order of the planets?

M V E M J S U N

____

____

Warm-Up 138

The Third Planet from the Sun

Name: ______________________________

We live on planet Earth. It is our home. Our home is huge and amazing, and it is full of life.

Earth is one of eight planets in our solar system. It is the third planet from the sun. Of the eight planets, Earth is the fifth-largest. It is the only planet that we know contains life.

From space, Earth looks mostly blue and white, with some brown areas, too. The blue is the ocean water. Ocean water makes up about 70% of Earth's surface. The white is the clouds that swirl above Earth. The brown is the land.

Ocean water has lots of salt in it. But Earth contains lots of fresh water, too. Water is the key to life. Earth is the only planet in our solar system that has water. It is also the only planet that has oxygen. Earth's plants produce oxygen. Oxygen is a gas that makes life possible for people and other forms of life on Earth. Oxygen has also helped create the ozone layer. This layer is high up in the sky, between Earth and the sun. The ozone layer blocks the parts of the sun's rays that are harmful for us and other animals. The ozone layer also helps keep temperatures from getting too hot.

What Did You Learn ?

Part 1 Directions: Look at the three colors listed below. They are the three colors of Earth that can be seen the most from space. Next to each word, write the part of Earth that is that color, as seen from space.

blue ________________ brown ________________ white ________________

Part 2 Directions: Look at the words in the box. Write them on the lines below to complete the sentence.

the sun	**ozone**	**oxygen**	**Earth**

On ______________________, plants produce ______________________.

This gas helps create the ______________________________ layer.

This layer protects us from the rays of ______________________________.

A Look Inside Our Planet

Name: ______________________________

Have you ever cut open an onion? An onion is made up of many layers. In this way, Earth is like an onion. It is made up of layers.

Earth is made up of four main layers. Each is very different.

- The outer layer of Earth is called the **crust**. It is solid, and it goes down as far as 30 miles (50 km) in some places. The ground we walk on is the very outer part of the crust.
- The layer below the crust is called the **mantle**. This layer can be up to 1,800 miles (2,900 km) thick. It is Earth's thickest layer.
- Next is the **outer core**. This layer is liquid. It is about 1,400 miles (2,250 km) thick. The temperature of this layer can reach up to 11,000°F (6,100°C).
- The innermost layer of Earth is the **inner core**. This layer is like a solid ball at the center of Earth.

Part 1 Directions: Label each layer of Earth.

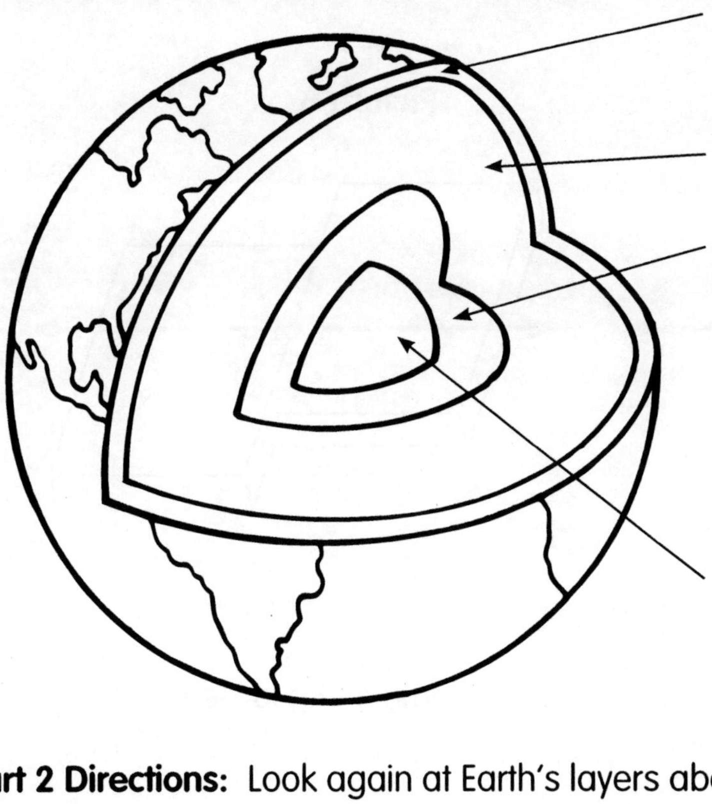

1. ______________________

2. ______________________

3. ______________________

4. ______________________

Part 2 Directions: Look again at Earth's layers above. Do the following:

- Find the layer that is the thickest. Write the word **THICK** in it.
- Find the area that is the most liquid. Write **LIQUID** in it.

Warm-Up 140

A Puzzle Made of Moving Pieces

Name: ________________________________

Have you ever felt an earthquake? Some earthquakes can be very mild. Others can really shake everything up and cause damage. Here's how earthquakes happen:

Earth is made up a few different layers. The top layer is made up of large pieces of rock. They are like the pieces of a puzzle. These puzzle pieces of rock are called **tectonic plates**. Tectonic plates are always moving and rubbing against each other. The edges of these plates get stuck together, but the rest of the rock piece keeps trying to move. This causes a lot of energy to build up. Sometimes the rock pieces suddenly become unstuck. They slip past each other. When they do this, all of that energy is released. The energy moves in waves, like ripples in a pool of water. The energy moves outward from the place where the two pieces slipped past each other. We feel these waves of energy as they ripple below us. We call this an earthquake.

Part 1 Directions: Look at the pictures. They both show two rock pieces that are stuck together. They both have arrows showing the direction **the energy moves**. Circle the one that shows the correct direction energy moves when the rock pieces become unstuck.

Picture A

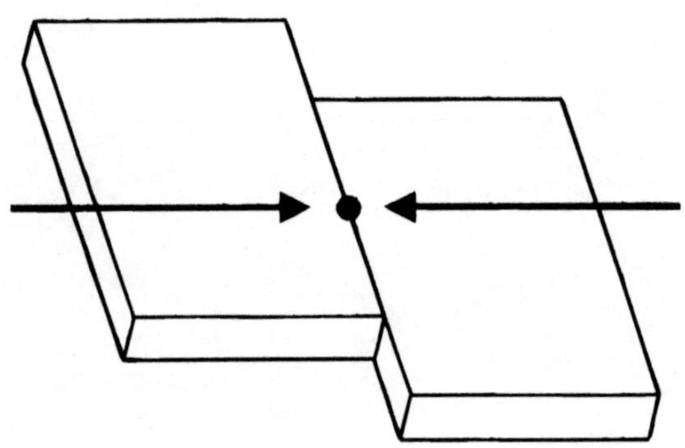

Picture B

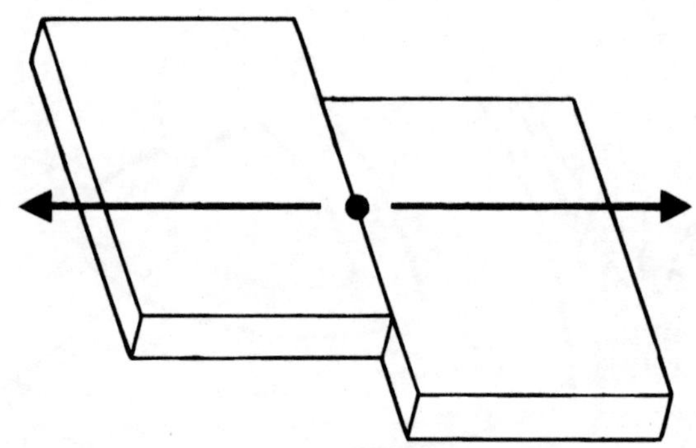

Part 2 Directions: Unscramble the letters to find the name of the large puzzle pieces of rock that form the outer layer of Earth.

____

C O T E N T I C   A P S L T E

Our Ever-Changing Earth

Name: ______________________________

Earth is always changing. Most of these changes happen so slowly that we never notice them. For example, a constant stream of water running over a large rock will change the rock. It will wear down the rock and make it smaller. This can take hundreds or thousands of years. This type of change is called *erosion*.

There are other changes we don't notice because they happen deep under the ground. There are large pieces of rock that form the outer layer of Earth. These pieces are always moving. If they move in a certain way, an earthquake can happen. This is one way Earth can change suddenly and quickly. A large earthquake can cause cracks in the ground, for example. Now think about a volcano that is erupting. Hot lava shoots out of the volcano and covers the ground. This lava cools and forms new rock. This changes the land on Earth.

Directions: Look at the timeline. Write examples of events that change Earth. For Sections #1 and #3, you can use examples from what you have just read. For Section #2, think of a good example of something that fits in between #1 and #3.

Quickest

Section #1

a change to Earth that happens suddenly

Section #2

a change to Earth that takes a while

Section #3

a change to Earth that happens very slowly

Slowest

Warm-Up 142

All the Days and Years on Earth

Name: ______________________________

It may not feel like it, but Earth is moving. For example, it is rotating, or spinning. It takes Earth about 24 hours to spin around once. That is the reason we have day and night. The side of Earth facing the sun has day. As Earth rotates, that side spins and no longer faces the sun. It becomes night on that side of Earth.

Earth is also moving around the sun as it rotates. In fact, it takes 365.25 days for Earth to make one complete trip *around* the sun. Does the number "365" sound familiar? That's how many days are in a year. (The ".25" at the end of "365.25" is important, too. Every four years, the ".25" adds up to "1." This is why we have a leap year every fourth year. Every leap year has 366 days in it.)

Part 1 Directions: Look at each picture. Answer the questions.

1.

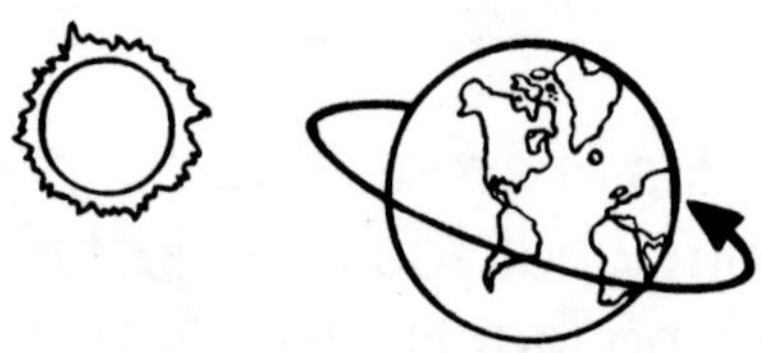

How long does it take for this to happen?

____

2.

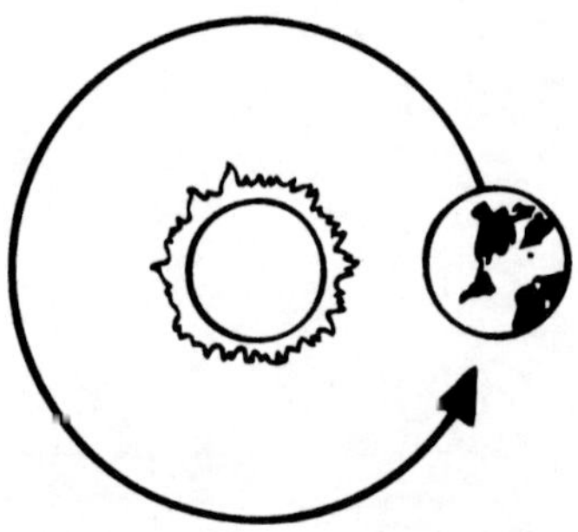

How long does it take for this to happen?

____

Part 2 Directions: Leap years occur every fourth year. In leap years, we have an extra day. In those years, we have the day of February 29. In other years, there is no February 29.

1. Do you know anyone whose birthday is February 29? ____________________

2. Would you like it if your birthday were on February 29? ____________________

Explain your answer. ____

____

____

What Is in the Air?

Warm-Up 143

Name: ______________________________

Everything we see and use is made up of elements. What are elements? They are like ingredients. Think of an apple pie. An apple pie is made up of ingredients like flour, sugar, cinnamon, and apples. Together, they make up the pie. To be just right, the pie needs only a little of some ingredients, like cinnamon. It needs a lot of other ingredients, like flour and apples.

But what makes up apples and pie pans and the air? There are about 100 basic elements on Earth that do this.

Directions: Look at the pie chart below. It shows the basic elements that make up the air on Earth. Use this information to answer the questions below.

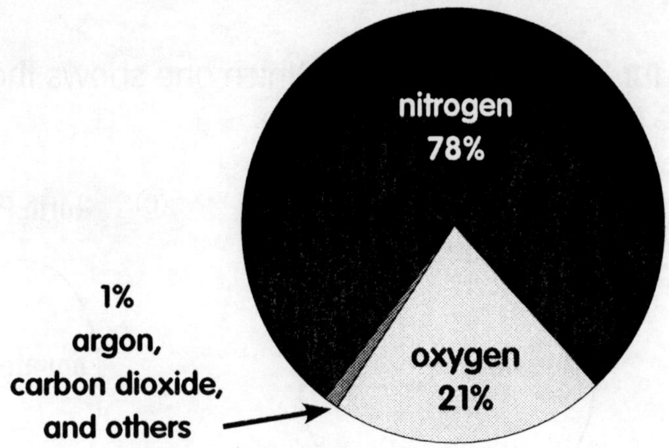

1. Which element makes up the largest part of air? ______________________

2. Which element makes up the second-largest part? ______________________

An analogy is a statement that compares things that are not alike. An example of an analogy would be this:

apples are to **apple pie** as **nitrogen** is to **the air**

In other words, apples are the main ingredient in apple pie, just like nitrogen is the main ingredient in the air.

Now complete this analogy. Fill in the circle of the best answer.

3. cinnamon is to **apple pie** as ____________ is to the **air**

Ⓐ nitrogen Ⓑ oxygen Ⓒ carbon dioxide

Unit 17 — Earth & Space Science: Earth

Some Facts About Earth

Name: ______________________________

How much do you know about the planet you live on? Here are some Earth facts:

- Earth is not perfectly round! It is a bit flattened at the North Pole and at the South Pole. It bulges a bit in the middle near the equator. This shape is called an *oblate spheroid.* (It's easier to just say "round"!)
- The highest point on Earth is at the top of Mount Everest. The peak of this mountain in Asia rises up 29,000 feet above sea level.
- The lowest point on Earth is at the bottom of Mariana Trench in the Pacific Ocean. It is over 36,000 feet below sea level. This means that Mariana Trench is deeper than Mount Everest is tall!

Part 1 Directions: Look at the three pictures below. Which one shows the basic shape of Earth. Fill in the circle next to the correct shape.

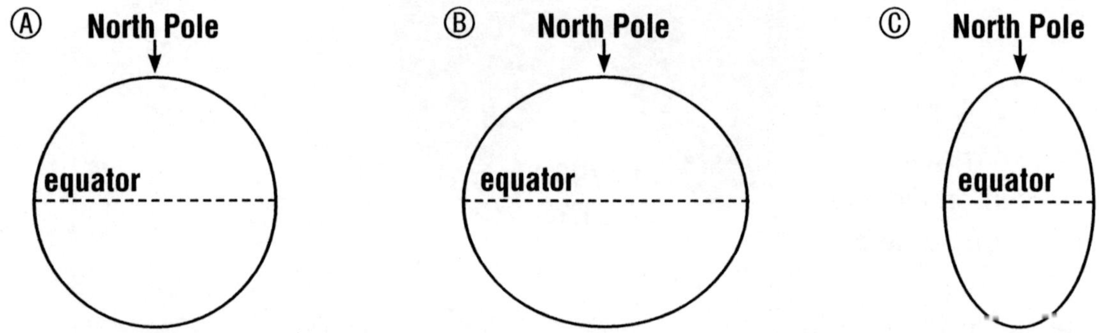

Part 2 Directions: Look at the picture below. Imagine that it is an invitation to visit the tallest mountain on Earth. Fill in the information needed on the lines. This will give the reader some of the information he or she needs to know about this very tall mountain.

____
(name of mountain)

____
(continent where mountain is located)

____
(height above sea level)

Word Study

Warm-Up 145

Name: ______________________________________

We have day and night because of how Earth rotates, or spins. When one side of Earth is facing the sun, it is day on that side of Earth. When that side is facing away from the sun, it is night there.

Day and night are very different. In fact, they are opposites!

Part 1 Directions: Each word on the left is the opposite of a word on the right. Draw lines to match each word on the left with its opposite on the right.

1. night	below
2. noon	day
3. north	inside
4. outside	midnight
5. above	south

Part 2 Directions: Each word on the left has about the same meaning as a word on the right. Draw lines to connect each word on the left with its matching word on the right.

1. Earth	12 p.m.
2. noon	12 a.m.
3. year	24 hours
4. day	365 days
5. midnight	world

Warm-Up 146

Life on a Rocky Planet

Name: ______________________________

Earth is a rocky planet. It is made of rock. Rocks are solid objects that are made up of minerals. But rocks can break down over time. The weather and other things cause rocks to break down. Rocks can then break all the way down until they become soil. Some people use the word *dirt* or *earth* (with a lowercase *e*) when they are talking about soil.

Soil is very important to Earth. Good soil has the right mixture of minerals. This mixture allows plants to grow in the soil. Without soil like this, we would not have enough food for the world to survive. Most animals eat plants, or they eat other animals that eat plants.

What Did You Learn ?

1. Which of these needs soil to grow?

   Ⓐ rocks   Ⓑ plants   Ⓒ minerals

2. What is one thing the story says can break down rocks?

   Ⓐ weather   Ⓑ minerals   Ⓒ soil

3. Which word is not another name for soil?

   Ⓐ dirt   Ⓑ earth   Ⓒ Earth

4. Look at the diagram. Use it to explain why soil is important to lions, even if they don't eat plants that grow in soil.

____

____

____

____

____

____

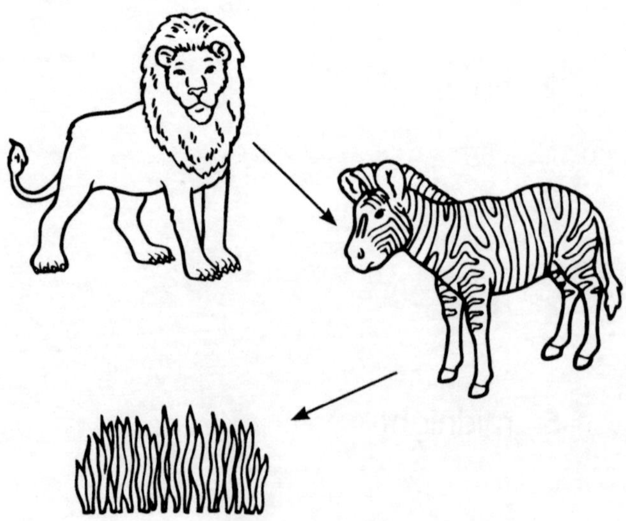

The Three Main Kinds of Rock

Warm-Up 147

Name: ______________________________

There are three main types of rocks: igneous, sedimentary, and metamorphic.

- **Igneous rocks** are formed when hot, liquid rock cools. The word *igneous* means "made from fire or heat." Where does liquid rock come from? It comes from inside Earth. It gets to the surface by coming out of volcanoes when they erupt. This liquid rock is called *lava*. When it cools, it becomes solid. That is when it becomes igneous rock.
- **Sedimentary rocks** are formed from sand, mud, or pebbles that pile up in the bottoms of rivers, streams, lakes, and ponds. These rocks got there by crumbling off of mountains and hills. Over many years, several layers of this kind of rock stack up on top of each other. The layers push down on top of each other. Many fossils are found in sedimentary rock for this reason. Animals and plants die and get stuck between the layers. This keeps them from getting worn away by sun, wind, and rain.
- **Metamorphic rocks** are formed when igneous or sedimentary rocks are changed because of heat or pressure from Earth. The word *metamorphic* means "to change form." These rocks are formed when Earth's outer layer moves a lot. This movement causes heat and pressure. The heat and pressure squeeze the rock so hard that it changes. Metamorphic rock is the least common type on Earth.

Directions: Look at the **Facts Box**. Which rock is being described by each fact? Write the number of the fact in the correct place to the right. The first one is done for you.

Facts Box

1. ~~least common type of rock~~
2. forms at bottoms of lakes
3. made when liquid rock cools
4. formed from sand and mud
5. often contains fossils
6. comes from volcanoes
7. rocks that have changed form
8. means "made from heat"

Igneous

Sedimentary

Metamorphic

1

Warm-Up 148

Rocks That Were Once Liquid

Name: ______________________________

Rocks are solid. But some started out as liquid. There is liquid rock deep under the ground. This liquid is called **magma**. It is very hot.

A **volcano** is like a mountain made of many layers of rock. The area at the top of a volcano is sunk in. This area is called a **crater**. There is a hole in the middle of the crater. Magma from deep underground can explode out of this hole. When the liquid comes out, it is called **lava**. Lava is very hot. The hot lava runs down the side of the volcano. Over time, it cools. What does it become once it cools? It becomes solid rock.

Part 1 Directions: Look at the picture of the volcano. Label each part. Use the **Volcano Words** box to help you.

Volcano Words		
crater	lava	magma

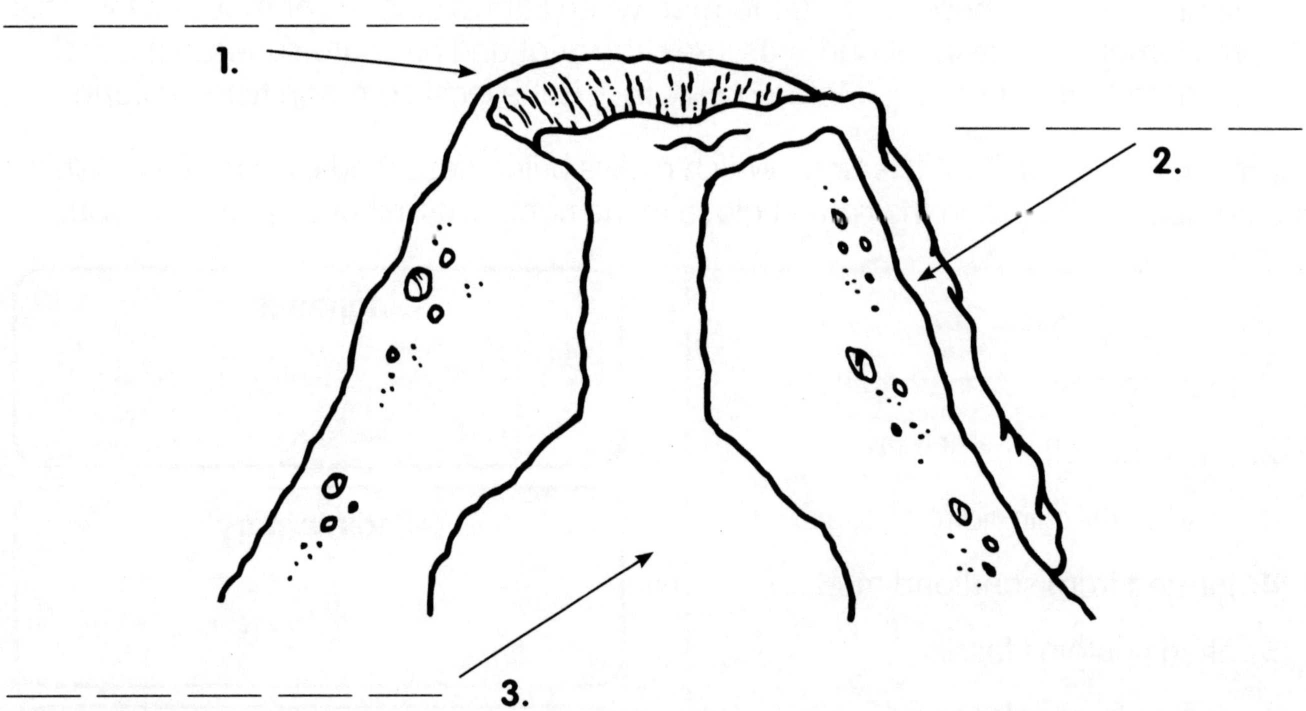

Part 2 Directions: Are these things solid or liquid? Write **S** next to the word if it is in solid form. Write **L** next to the word if it is in liquid form.

lava ______________ magma ______________ rock ______________

What Rocks Can Do

Name: ______________________________

Rocks are all around us. They are also in a lot of things we make. We use rocks in a lot of ways.

Many things can be built from rocks. We build walls and other strong things with rocks. There are even famous landmarks built of rock. One is called Mount Rushmore. This landmark shows the faces of four U.S. presidents. Their faces are carved into the rock of the mountain.

There are many uses for crushed rocks, too. We crush the rocks into small pieces. We use this to make gravel and cement. Some people fill their driveways with gravel. Most sidewalks and curbs are made from cement.

Rocks are not living things. Sometimes, though, things that were once living can be found in rocks. These things are called *fossils*. Rocks are very hard, and they don't fall apart easily. This keeps fossils in good condition for a long time. We can learn about the past by looking at these fossils.

Directions: Read each statement. If it is true, color the rock **brown**. If it is false, draw an **X** through the rock.

1. Gravel is a form of crushed rock.
2. Rocks are living things.
3. People use rocks to build things.
4. Rocks need water to live.
5. Fossils can be found in rocks.
6. Cement is made of rock.
7. Rocks can help us learn about the past.
8. Mount Rushmore shows the faces of five U.S. presidents.

Warm-Up 150

Why Soil Is So Important

Name: ______________________________

What do you see when you look at a garden? You may notice the beautiful flowers. You may see rows of delicious vegetables and fruits. But none of these things can grow without good soil. Good soil is filled with minerals. Good soil is moist. This means that it has water in it. The soil and the water give nutrients to the plants. Without good soil, we would not be able to grow food for us to eat.

Can you think of some foods that grow from soil? Think of potatoes. They grow under the soil. We dig them out of the soil when they are ready to be eaten. Other foods like carrots, beats, and peanuts also grow under the soil.

Many foods grow up from the soil. They grow as plants. Tomatoes, corn, and lettuce grow this way. Many fruits—like apples, oranges, and lemons—grow on trees. All of these plants and trees have roots. The roots go deep into the soil. They bring minerals from the soil to the plants.

Directions: Build your own garden! Do the following:

- Draw one food that grows under the soil.
- Draw a plant that is growing one type of food.
- Draw a tree that is growing one type of fruit.

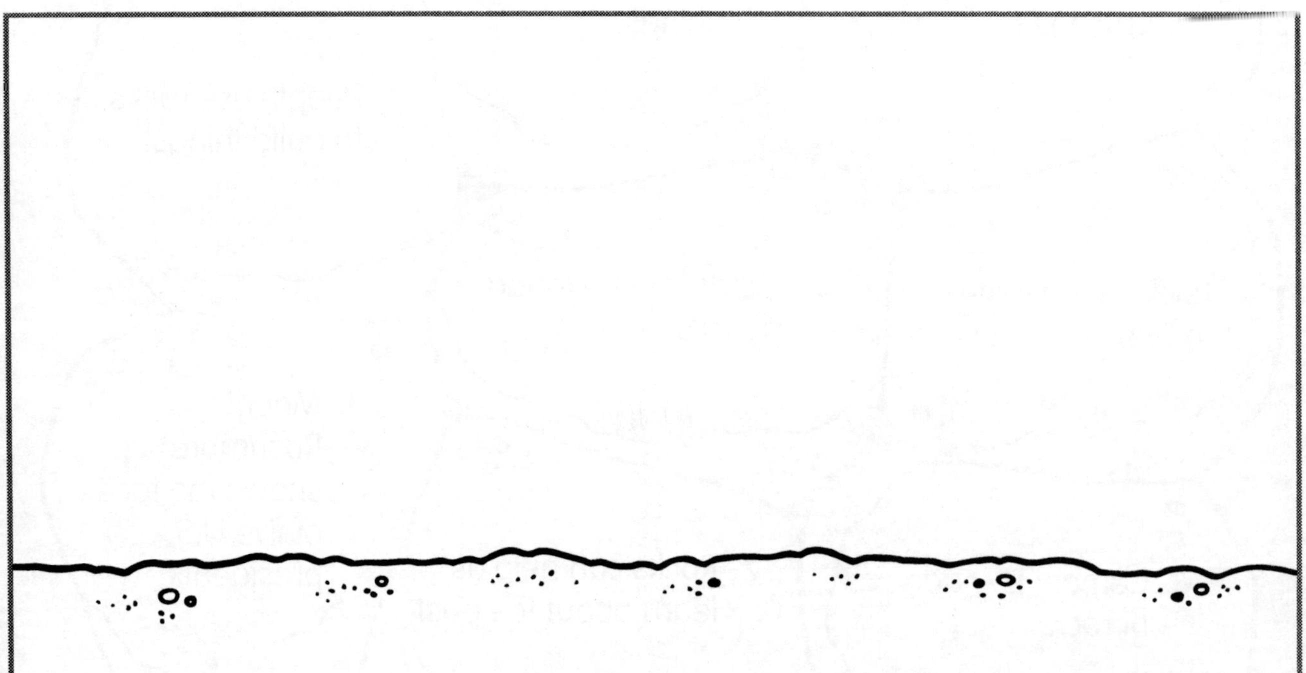

All About Sand

Name: ____

Have you ever been to a sandy beach? Have you ever sunk your toes into soft, warm sand? Would it surprise you to know that sand is mostly made of rock? The pieces of rock have been worn down. They are very small. It does not feel as if you are walking on rocks at all.

The sand at the beach might also have shells and bits of coral in it. Those materials are worn down, too. The waves from the ocean form the sand at the beach. These waves carry the rocks, shells, and coral to the shore. They break down these materials until they are very small. A grain of sand is less than 2 millimeters long. That's small!

Deserts have sand, too. This sand is carried there by the wind. Some deserts were formed where lakes or seas used to be. The water is long gone, but the sand is still there.

Part 1 Directions: Put these statements in order to show how sand gets on the beach. Write a **1** next to the thing that happens first. Write a **4** next to the thing that happens last.

________________ Tiny pieces of rock are left on the shore.

________________ Rocks from deep on the ocean floor come loose.

________________ Waves bring very small rocks to the shore.

________________ Rocks get smaller as they travel through the ocean.

Part 2 Directions: Six small pieces of rock have been measured. The measurements are written below. Only two of them can be called "sand." Only two of them are the right size. Circle the two that could be called "sand."

20 millimeters	**12 millimeters**	**½ millimeters**
3 millimeters	**1 millimeter**	**2 ½ millimeters**

Warm-Up 152

What's That Ring Made Of?

Name: ______________________________

Minerals are solid materials. All of the land on Earth rests on a layer of rock made up of minerals. Minerals also make up a lot of things you see and use every day.

Some minerals are made up of just one element. Some of these minerals are very valuable. We make rings and jewelry out of some of them.

Other minerals are made up of more than one element. We use these minerals for a lot of things, too.

Directions: Look at the rings below. Start with any letter. Follow the arrows. Does it form a word? If not, start at another letter. When you find a word (mineral name), copy the letters in order. Then, write one thing that mineral makes you think of.

		Name of Mineral	**What You Think Of**
1.	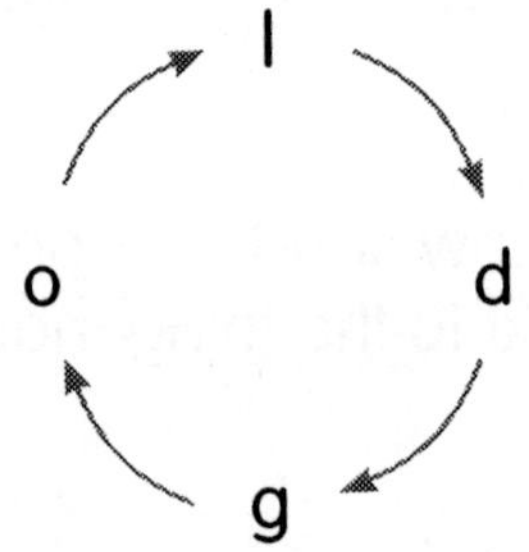	____________	____________ ____________
2.	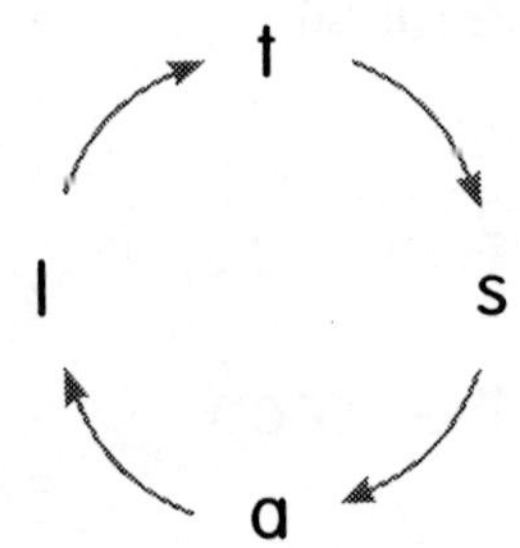	____________	____________ ____________
3.	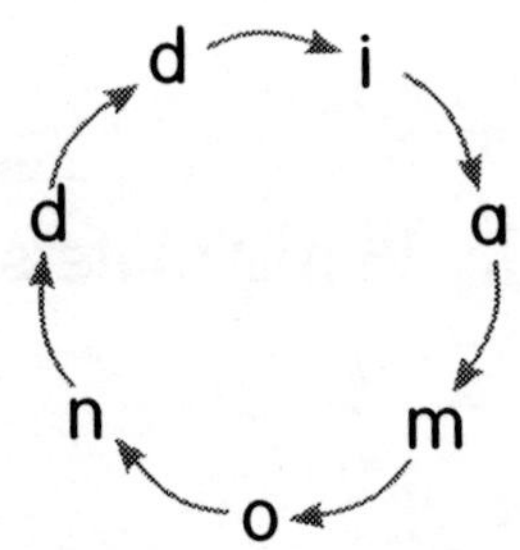	____________	____________ ____________

Warm-Up 153

Name: ______________________________

There are a lot of words we use to say "rock" or "soil." Let's look at some of them.

If we are talking about a really big rock, we call it a **boulder**. A small rock is called a **pebble**.

We often call soil by the word **dirt**. If it's the soft stuff we find at the beach or in the desert, it is called **sand**. When soil is really wet, we call it **mud**. We even call soil by the same name as our planet (Earth). But when we call soil **earth**, we use a lowercase *e*.

Directions: Look at the darkened words in the story above. Find each one in the word search below. Circle each word. The first one has been done for you.

M	P	E	B	B	L	E
D	I	R	T	I	N	A
B	O	U	L	D	E	R
E	R	M	U	D	A	T
S	A	N	D	L	S	H

Words to Find

~~boulder~~
dirt
earth
mud
pebble
sand

Challenge: Some of the letters in the word search are not circled. Write down those letters in order. They spell out the answer to this question:

What are rocks and soil mostly made of?

____ ____ ____ ____ ____ ____ ____ ____

Warm-Up 154

Let's Talk About the Weather

Name: ______________________________

The weather and the seasons play important roles in our lives. We need to know what the weather will be like each day. We need to dress in warm clothes when the weather is cold. We need to drink lots of water and wear sunscreen when the weather is very hot.

One way we know what to expect from the weather is by knowing what season it is. There are four seasons per year. They are spring, summer, autumn, and winter. Summers are usually hot, and winters are cold. The days are longer in the summer, and they are shorter in the winter. When the winter weather begins to warm up and the days begin to get longer, that is when we have spring. When the summer weather begins to cool down and the days begin to get shorter, that is when we have autumn.

We can't always guess the weather by the season, however. This is when a meteorologist can help. A meteorologist is a scientist who knows how to study the weather. He or she can tell if it will rain soon. He or she can tell us if the weather will soon get hot.

What Did You Learn ?

1. Which season comes after winter?

Ⓐ spring Ⓑ summer Ⓒ autumn

2. Which is **not** true about spring?

Ⓐ The days are longer than they are in winter.
Ⓑ The days are longer than they are in summer.

3. What is one fact about summer?

Ⓐ Earth is closest to the sun during summer.
Ⓑ The days are longest during summer.

What Am I ?

I am a scientist who studies the weather. What am I called?

___ e ___ e o ___ o ___ o ___ i ___ ___

Which Season Do You See?

Warm-Up 155

Name: ____________________________

The year is divided into four seasons: winter, spring, summer, and autumn. Winter is the coldest, and summer is the warmest. Spring is often the time when plants grow and animals are born. In autumn, the leaves fall off of the trees, and animals begin to prepare for the coming winter.

Directions: Look at each picture. Which season does it show? Write **winter, spring, summer**, or **autumn** on the line below each picture. Which season do you see?

1.

____

2.

____

3.

____

4.

____

Warm-Up 156

Different Places, Different Seasons

Name: ______________________________

When it is summer, the weather is usually hot. Everyone wears shorts and tries to stay cool. That is, everyone in your half of the world.

Earth faces the sun, but it is tilted. It is at an angle. This means that more sun hits one half of Earth as it spins. Each half of Earth is called a *hemisphere*.

The Northern Hemisphere of Earth gets more sun during half of the year. The Southern Hemisphere of Earth gets more sun during the other half. So when it is summer in the Northern Hemisphere, it is winter in the Southern Hemisphere. And when it is summer in the Southern Hemisphere, it is winter in the Northern. The seasons are always opposite each other.

Directions: Look at the chart. It shows the seasons in each hemisphere. Use what you have learned to complete the chart.

	Northern Hemisphere	**Southern Hemisphere**
January	winter	summer
April	spring	autumn
June		winter
October	autumn	

Now write your birthday here:

____

In what season would your birthday be

- in the Northern Hemisphere? ______________________________
- in the Southern Hemisphere? ______________________________

Today's Rain Has Been Here Before

Name: ______________________________

Earth has the same amount of water now as it had long ago. The water keeps getting used and coming back again. How can that be? It's all to do with something called the **water cycle**. This cycle has four main parts:

1. **evaporation** — The sun heats up the water in the oceans, lakes, and rivers. It turns the water into steam. The steam goes into the air.
2. **condensation** — Steam in the air gets cold. It turns into liquid and forms clouds.
3. **precipitation** — This happens when there is a lot of water in the air. The clouds get heavy. Water falls back to the ground as rain or snow.
4. **collection** — Some of the water from rain and snow runs back into the oceans, lakes, and rivers. The warm sun hits this water, and the cycle begins again.

Directions: Look at the picture. It shows the water cycle. Add the numbers from above to name each part. The first one has been done for you.

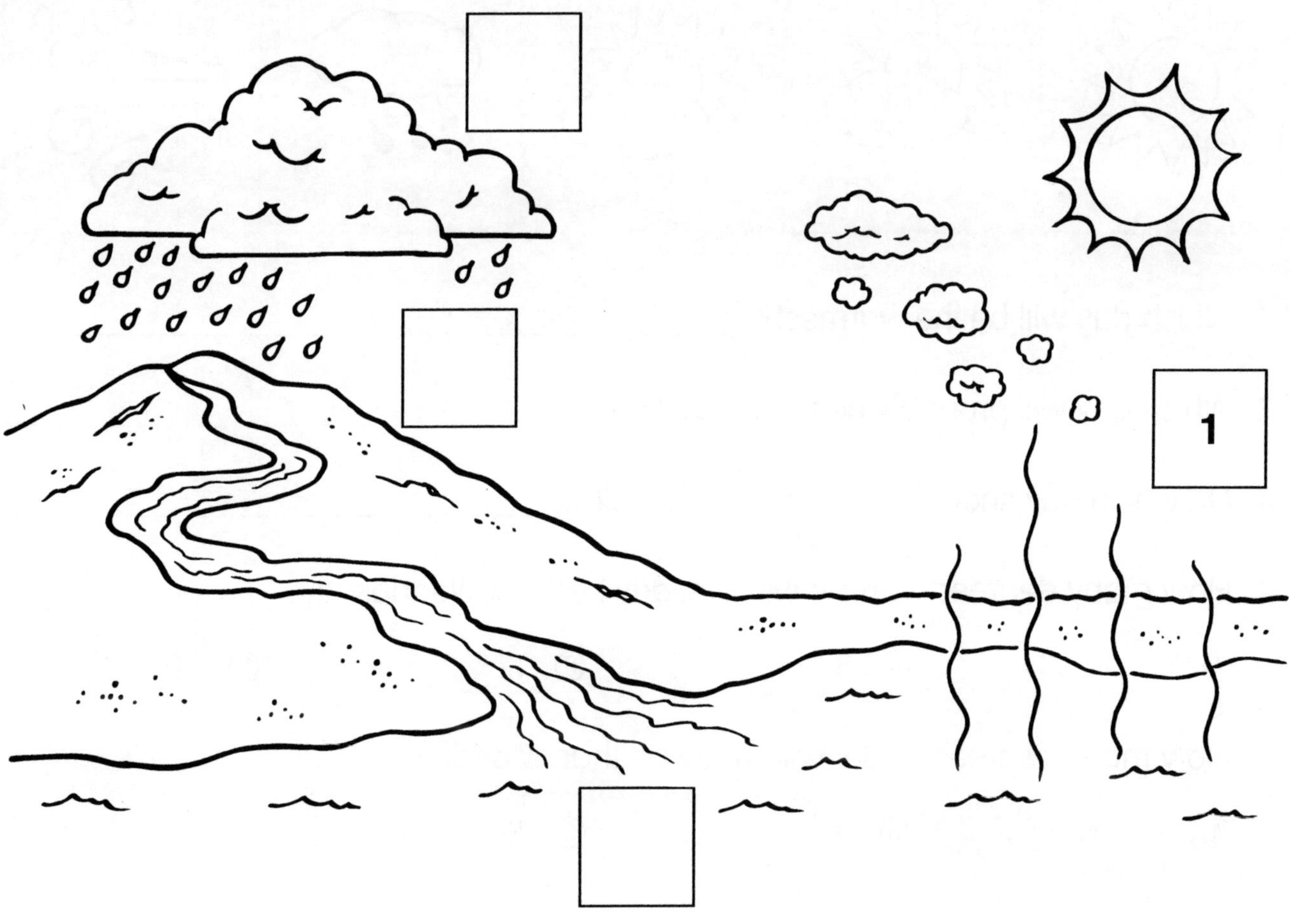

Warm-Up 158

Reading a Weather Forecast

Name: ______________________________

Let's say you have a fun trip planned in two days. You are worried that it might rain and ruin your fun. You would like to know what the weather will be like on that day. That is where the weather forecast can help you. It tells you what the weather will most likely be on that day.

Weather forecasts are not always right. But weather scientists do their best to give us the best guess possible. They use technology to figure out what kind of weather is coming our way.

Directions: The chart below shows a forecast for five days. It shows the temperatures. Higher temperatures mean hotter weather. Lower temperatures mean colder weather. The picture also tells us something. See what this chart tells you.

Monday	Tuesday	Wednesday	Thursday	Friday
72° 	65° 	60° 	51° 	52° 

1. Which day will be the warmest? ______________________________

2. Which day will probably be the coldest? ______________________________

3. On which day should you carry an umbrella? ______________________________

4. How many degrees warmer will Tuesday be than Wednesday?

   Ⓐ 5 Ⓑ 8 Ⓒ 12 Ⓓ 20

5. How many degrees colder will Friday be than Monday?

   Ⓐ 5 Ⓑ 8 Ⓒ 12 Ⓓ 20

All Kinds of Clouds

Name: ____________________________________

Not all clouds are the same. The clouds in a clear, sunny sky look different than the clouds in a stormy sky. Some clouds are puffy. Some seem to cover the whole sky.

Here are some different kinds of clouds:

- **Cirrus** clouds look like feathers.
- **Nimbostratus** clouds cover the sky like a dark gray sheet.
- **Cumulus** clouds are puffy. They look like clumps of cotton.

Directions: Draw lines to match each picture to its cloud name.

1.  **cirrus**

2.  **cumulus**

3.  **nimbostratus**

Which cloud do you think is most likely to bring rain? ____________________

Explain your answer. ____________________________________

____

Name: ______________________________

Part 1 Directions: Look at the word **TORNADO**. Can you find three small words spelled in order within **TORNADO**?

TORNADO ______________ ______________ ______________

Part 2 Directions: Look at the word **HAIL**. Can you change one letter at a time to make HAIL into RAIN? Each step must be a real word.

HAIL → ______________ → **RAIN**

Part 3 Directions: The wind blows things around. Imagine that the wind could blow letters away. Think about the word **BLOWING**. What if the wind blew away the letter **L**? The word that would be left would be **BOWING**. Then, if the wind blew the **B** away, the new word would be **OWING**.

Imagine that the wind keeps blowing one letter away at a time. Each time, it leaves behind a real word. Even when there is one letter left, it still makes a real word. See if you can figure out which letter is blown away each time.

BLOWING

BOWING

OWING

____

____

____

____

Answer Key

Unit 1

The World of the Living (page 7)

1. A
2. B
3. D
4. >
5. <

Separate the Living from the Non-Living (page 8)

P	C	C	M	U	C	Z	O	W	L
O	A	L	J	Q	O	R	S	T	U
F	R	O	G	L	M	P	Y	D	U
L	V	C	S	S	P	I	D	E	R
E	A	K	K	L	U	Z	Z	S	A
P	P	L	A	N	T	Z	E	K	V
W	M	M	O	Q	E	A	U	N	G
A	G	R	Y	T	R	E	E	J	A

Living Things		Non-Living Things	
frog	spider	car	desk
owl	tree	clock	pizza
plant		computer	

A Walk in the Park (page 9)
Living Things: tree, butterfly, boy, dog, flowers, grass, bird, squirrel
Non-Living Things: bench, drinking fountain, sign, trashcan, leash

The Life Cycle of a Ladybug (page 10)

1. eggs (should be colored pale yellow)
2. larva (should be colored black and yellow or orange)
3. pupa (should be colored bright yellow)
4. adult (should be colored bright red with black spots)

The Creature That Does Not Die (page 11)
Accept appropriate responses.

The Stages of Your Life (page 12)
Accept appropriate responses.

Match the Parents with Their Children (page 13)

1. d
2. a
3. c
4. e
5. b
6. 1. human baby; 2. puppy; 4. chick
7. 3. caterpillar; 5. tadpole

Passed Down from Your Parents (page 14)

Part 1

1. I
2. L
3. L
4. L
5. I
6. L
7. I
8. I
9. I
10. L

Part 2
Accept appropriate responses.

Word Study (page 15)

Part 1
Plants: fern, mint, moss, pine, oak
Insects: beetle, locust, mantis, termite, cricket
Vertebrates: crocodile, gorilla, halibut, pelican, elephant

Part 2
Accept appropriate responses.

Unit 2

A Place to Live and Grow (page 16)

1. D
2. C
3. B

What Am I?: sunlight

Animals and Their Habitats (page 17)

1. whale
2. camel
3. crocodile
4. monkey

Finding Just the Right Place (page 18)

1. polar bear – Place B
2. tarantula – Place C
3. toucan – Place A

Warm and Wet and Full of Life (page 19)

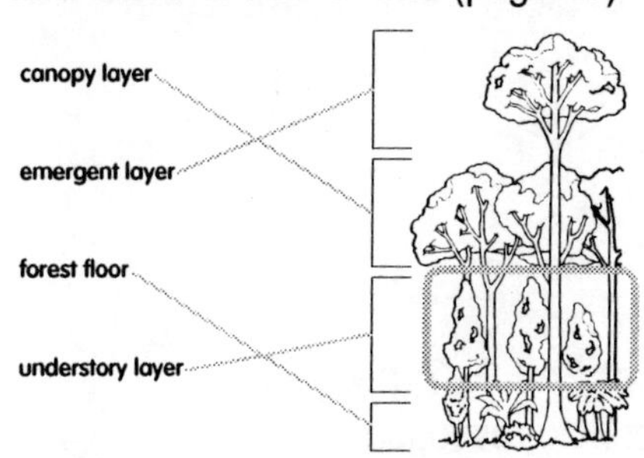

Some Like It Hot, and Here's Why (page 20)

1. humps
2. coat
3. cells
4. nostrils
5. lashes

When the Weather Turns Cold (page 21)
3, 5, 1, 4, 2

What's for Dinner? (page 22)

1. C
2. O
3. H
4. O
5. H
6. C

The Parts of a Food Chain (page 23)
Boxes should be glued in this order, from left to right:
plant, caterpillar, frog, snake, owl

It's Gross, It's Green, and It's Alive! (page 24)
These four pieces of bread should be colored green:
dark, open to the air, warm, wet

Word Study (page 25)

1. habitat
2. termites
3. Antarctica
4. box jellyfish
5. tapeworm

Unit 3

Insects Are Everywhere! (page 26)

1. D
2. B
3. A (Chart A is the only chart that shows that more than half of all living things are insects.)

Finish the Picture (page 27)
Check drawings for accuracy.

Insect or Not? (page 28)

1. I
2. N
3. N
4. I
5. N
6. I

Pets, Pests, or Snacks? (page 29)
Accept appropriate responses.

A Job for Every Ant (page 30)

1. male — drones
   female — workers, soldiers, queen
2. drone — dies young; queen — starts colony;
   soldier — big jaws; worker — many jobs

Quick Quiz: queen ant

Be as Busy as a Bee (page 31)

The Deadliest Animal on Earth (page 32)

1. Africa (Asia or Latin America are also acceptable answers.)
2. dragonfly
3. All animals should be circled.

Word Study (page 33)

Part 1
butterfly, earwig, grasshopper, ladybug, silkworm

Part 2
Accept appropriate responses.

Unit 4

There Are Many Fish (and Other Animals) in the Sea (page 34)

1. C
2. A
3. crocodile — reptile; shark — fish;
   squid — invertebrate; whale — mammal

What Am I?: salt water

Water, Water All Around (page 35)

Part 1
Section A should be colored blue.
Answer: C, more than half

Part 2
Section A: shark, octopus, dolphin, crab, jellyfish
Section B: pig, bee

Answer Key

The Creatures of the Coral Reefs (page 36)

Brain Coral — purple
Butterfly Fish — blue
Elkhorn Coral — purple
Lettuce Leaf Sea Slug — red
Octopus — red
Queen Angelfish — blue
Seafans — purple
Sea Horse — blue
Sea Star — red

One Feared Fish (page 38)

1. These descriptions should be crossed out: plant-eaters; dull, flat teeth; eyes like other fish; not good at hunting; won't attack humans
2. B
3. 3,000

There's No Place Like Home (page 39)

Point A — fresh
Point B — salt
Point C — fresh

Underwater-Animal Math (page 40)

1. 5 + 10 = 15
2. 4 + 3 = 7
3. 8 – 2 = 6
4. 10 – 8 = 2
5. 100 + 0 = 100

Word Study (page 43)

1. C
2. B
3. D
4. A

Unit 5

This Land Is Our Land...and Theirs, Too (page 44)

1. A
2. C
3. cat, 3; elephant, 6; horse, 5; mouse, 2; person, 4; spider, 1

Getting Around on Land (page 45)

Accept reasonable responses.

Mammals and More (page 46)

Mammals (brown)— dog, pig, cow, mouse

Reptiles (green)— crocodile, lizard, snake

Amphibians (yellow)— frog, newt, salamander

Invertebrates (orange)— worm, spider, fly

The word *reptile* should be circled.

All Kinds of Coverings (page 47)

Feathers: ostrich, peacock, turkey
Fur: lion, polar bear, wolf
Scales: lizard, snake
Shells: snail, turtle

Which Land Animal Is Which? (page 48)

1. frog
2. slug
3. crocodile
4. tortoise
5. mouse

Trace the Snakes...If You Dare! (page 49)

Snake #1 – Cobra (red)
Snake #2 – Rattlesnake (green)
Snake #3 – Black Mamba (black)
Snake #4 – Boa Constrictor (orange)

The Trouble with Long Legs (page 50)

1. C
2. Helpful: kicking enemies
   Not Helpful: drinking water, walking
3. A and D

Word Study (page 51)

1. lion
2. worm
3. bear
4. rabbit
5. snail
6. elephant
7. penguin
8. mouse
9. monkey
10. panda
11. armadillo
12. porcupine

Unit 6

How Do They Get Up There? (page 52)

1. D
2. A
3. C

Part 2

The arrow should be pointing down.

Taking Turns at the Front (page 53)

Blue circle — around the last two birds
Red square — around the bird in front
More birds — two birds drawn behind the back row

Some Birds Cannot Fly (page 54)

1. false, flying, flightless
2. true
3. false, flier, swimmer
4. true
5. false, animal, bird
6. false, Africa, Australia
7. true
8. false, fewer, more

Surprise, These Creatures Can Fly! (page 55)

1.

Lizard	Squirrel	*Snake*	Fish
30 feet	*150 feet*	330 feet	*650 feet*

Riders on the Wind (page 56)

Part 1

1. B
2. D
3. C

Part 2: wingspan

The Teeny-Tiny, Backwards-Flying Bird (page 57)

1. D
2. B
3. A
4. up through 16 should be shaded

Birds of a Feather... (page 58)

1. pod
2. flight
3. band
4. raft
5. kettle
6. murder

Word Study (page 59)

1. soaring
2. fluttering
3. hovering
4. swooping
5. flapping
6. gliding

Unit 7

They Come in All Shapes and Sizes (page 60)

1. B
2. C
3. D
4. jellyfish — dangerous; blue lobster — unusual; blue whale — gentle

The Long, Slow Life of a Tortoise (page 61)

1. False
2. True
3. True
4. False

Part 2

horse — 1st; fly — 3rd; pig — 2nd

The Long and the Short of It (page 62)

1. the longest fish
2. the shortest lizard
3. the longest lizard

What Am I?: stick

Never Challenge a Cheetah to a Race (page 63)

1. spine
2. tail
3. body
4. claws
5. nostrils

Nature's Best Jumpers (page 64)

1. 5
2. 20
3. 100
4. 150
5. 220

Use Your Clues (page 65)

1. A giraffe has a very long neck, so it needs to pump its blood at a high pressure so the blood can reach its brain.
2. Birds of prey fly very high above the ground, so they need great eyesight in order to see their food source (small rodents) crawling on the ground below.

Word Study (page 67)

1. C
2. B
3. scent
4. teeth
5. claws
6. hair

Unit 8

The Problems Animals Can Face (page 68)

1. B
2. D
3. Answers will vary. Students should mention that a type of animal will die out if too many die and not enough babies are produced to keep the species going.

Answer Key

How Animals Become Endangered (page 69)

1. B
2. A
3. C
4. A
5. D

The Mystery of the "Terrible Lizards" (page 70)
Students should write "Terrible Lizard" on the dinosaur, draw a volcano next to the dinosaur, and write "meteorite" above it.

The Last Ones of Their Kind (page 71)
dodo – 1662
great auk – 1852
quagga – 1883
passenger pigeon – 1914
Caribbean monk seal – 1952
golden toad – 1989
western black rhinoceros – 2011

Fossils: Clues About the Past (page 72)
4, 2, 5, 1, 3

Which Fossil Did You Find? (page 73)

1. bone
2. tooth
3. shell
4. insect
5. footprint
6. bone or tooth

Surviving in the Wild (page 74)

1. rattlesnake — The scary sound warns other animals to stay away.
2. puffer fish — It can suddenly look as if it is much bigger than it really is.
3. opossum — Other creatures think this animal is dead, so they leave it alone.
4. monarch butterfly — The food they eat makes them taste terrible to other animals.

Word Study (page 75)
"winged lizard" = *Pteranosaurus*
"terrible lizard" = *Tyrannosaurus*
"three-horned head" = *Triceratops*
"egg thief" = *Oviraptor*
"speedy thief" = *Velociraptor*

Unit 9

The Important Lives of Plants (page 76)

1. A
2. D
3. D

What Am I?: photosynthesis

We Need Each Other (page 77)
Arrow #1: carbon dioxide
Arrow #2: oxygen

The Basic Parts of a Plant (page 78)

1. flower
2. stem
3. leaf
4. roots

Plant Parts on Our Plates (page 79)

1. leaf
2. root
3. fruit
4. flower
5. seeds
6. leaf
7. fruit
8. flower
9. root

A Plant's Life (page 80)
clockwise from top left: 4, 1, 3, 5, 2, 6

Comparing Apples to Oranges (page 81)

1. C
2. C
3. B
4. A
5. A
6. A
7. B
8. B

T-Shirts and Ketchup and So Much More (page 82)
plants should be matched to products as follows:
cacao plant: chocolate bar, hot cocoa
cotton plant: T-shirt, blanket
peppermint plant: toothpaste, candy cane
tomato plant: ketchup, spaghetti sauce
tree: doghouse, baseball bat
wheat: bread, cereal

'Tis the Season to Lose Leaves (page 83)

Note: Answers are based on seasons in the Northern Hemisphere.

1. Circle the tree losing leaves.
2. Circle the tree with leaves.
3. Circle the tree losing leaves.
4. Circle the tree with leaves.
5. Circle the tree with leaves.
6. Circle the tree losing leaves.

Which of the Three Do You See? (page 84)

Accept appropriate responses.

Word Study (page 85)

1. roots
2. trunk
3. leaves
4. rings
5. stump
6. branch

Unit 10

All Systems Go! (page 86)

1. C
2. B
3. A
4. <

Your Hard-Working Heart (page 87)

1. B
2. A
3. A

What Am I?: valve

Are You in Your Right Mind? (page 88)

Accept appropriate responses.

With a Little Help from Your Friend (page 89)

1. your leg
2. your ear
3. a baby

Think About It!: Accept appropriate responses.

Three of Each (page 90)

Part 1

1. tibia – leg
2. molar – mouth
3. cerebellum – brain
4. radius – arm
5. incus – ear

Part 2

humerus

Making Sense of Your Senses (page 91)

Accept appropriate responses.

What Happens in the Blink of an Eye (page 92)

Number of Minutes	1	2	3	4	5	10
Average Person	15	30	45	**60**	75	150
Young Baby	2	**4**	6	**8**	10	**20**
Computer User	7	14	**21**	28	**35**	70

1. A
2. C
3. C

A Matter of Taste (page 93)

Part 1

1. C 2. B

Part 2

T	A	L	T	Y	S	O
S	E	U	R	M	W	L
O	B	I	T	T	E	R
U	S	L	A	E	E	K
R	P	S	A	L	T	Y

What Gives You Goose Bumps? (page 94)

Part 1: 3, 2, 4, 1

Part 2: The porcupine should be circled

Things That Grow and Grow (page 96)

1. 12 inches
2. December (if living in Northern Hemisphere)
3.

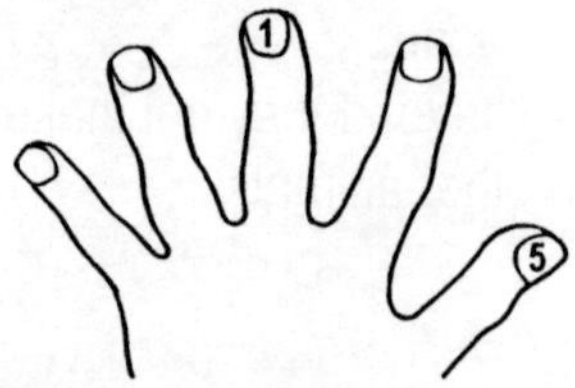

Word Study (page 97)

Part 1

1. knee
2. ankle
3. nose
4. stomach
5. thumb
6. finger
7. mouth

Part 2

Accept appropriate responses.

Answer Key

Unit 11

The Importance of Good Health (page 98)

1. C
2. A
3. A

What Am I?: doctor

Nature's Perfect Drink (page 99)

1. *circled:* person running, sick person
2. *circled:* apple, celery

Burning Calories (page 101)

1. B 2. B 3. C

How Much Sleep Do You Need? (page 102)

1. 14
2. 8
3. Answers may vary.
4. B
5. We need more sleep when we are younger. (Accept reasonable responses.)

An Army on the Inside (page 103)

Part 1: The neck, armpits, and knees should be circled.

Part 2: Line 1: immune system; Line 2: white

Word Study (page 105)

1. audiologist — ears and hearing
2. cardiologist — heart
3. dentist — teeth
4. dermatologist — skin
5. gastroenterologist — stomach
6. podiatrist — feet and ankles
7. immunologist — immune system

Unit 12

A World Built on Ideas (page 106)

1. B 2. C

How Scientists Must Think (page 107)

Colored bubbles:

Use the senses to observe.
Do experiments.
Run tests and get results.
Check results over and over again.

Bubbles with an X:

Find results once and quit looking.
Ignore the results that you don't like.
Make a guess and pretend that it's correct.

A Light That Keeps Glowing (page 109)

carbon

Who Invented What? (page 110)

Tim Berners-Lee – Internet
Philo Farnsworth – television
Guglielmo Marconi – radio
Charles Strite – pop-up toaster
Lester Wire – electric traffic light

Failures That Became Successes (page 111)

The following should be crossed out.

1. became successful right away
2. invented by Ruth Fry
3. discovered by an American scientist

Word Study (page 112)

1. botanist
2. zoologist
3. geologist
4. physicist
5. linguist
6. cytologist

Unit 13

What's the Matter? (page 113)

1. A
2. C
3. B
4. The ice has shape because it is a solid.

As a Matter of Fact (page 115)

1. solid
2. solid
3. liquid
4. liquid
5. gas
6. gas
7. solid
8. gas

Liquids and Solids (page 116)

1. the milk — liquid; the carton — solid
2. the bottle — solid; the juice — liquid
3. the cup — solid; the water — liquid
4. the oil — liquid; the can — solid
5. the bowl — solid; the water — liquid; the fish — solid

Getting Back in Shape (page 117)

1. yes
2. no
3. no
4. yes
5. no

All Shook Up and Nowhere to Go (page 118)

1. solid
2. The juice does not have carbon dioxide in it.

Answer Key

Word Study (page 119)

1. ape
2. car
3. ox
4. tea
5. one
6. ice
7. air
8. table
9. tree

Unit 14

Everything Is in Motion (page 120)

1. D
2. A
3. D

Challenge: False, but accept all responses that show critical thinking.

What's Truly on the Move? (page 121)

1. true (colored car)
2. false (x)
3. false (x)
4. true (colored car)
5. true (colored car)

What Goes Up Must Come Down (page 122)

1. C
2. C
3. A
4. B

Red Light, Green Light (page 123)

1. green
2. red
3. red
4. green

The Science of Making Waves (page 124)

1. wind
2. friction
3. gravity

The Push and Pull of Force (page 125)

1. pull
2. push
3. push
4. pull
5. pull
6. push

The Most Simple of Machines (page 126)

1. lever
2. wedge
3. wheel
4. inclined plane

Word Study (page 127)

Verbs: played, hit, stole, pitched, caught, cheered

Unit 15

Our Lives Are Full of Energy (page 128)

Part 1: All pictures should be circled.

Part 2: Picture should be of the sun.

Plugging in to Electricity (page 129)

The word "current" should be circled because the picture shows electricity that moves from one place (the wall socket) to another (the refrigerator).

Have You Heard About This? (page 130)

1. B
2. C
3. A

Lightning, Then Thunder (page 131)

Story #2, because the narrator saw the crash first and then heard it.

You and Your Shadow (page 132)

1. yes
2. no
3. no
4. yes

Attracted or Not? (page 134)

Colored: paper clip, fish hook, screw, spoon
Crossed out: pencil, football, glass, book

Word Study (page 135)

1. sound
2. plants
3. sleep
4. fossil
5. magnet
6. heat

Unit 16

Space and Everything in It (page 136)

Part 1

1. true
2. false
3. false
4. true
5. false

Part 2

big = planet
bigger = solar system
biggest = galaxy

Answer Key

The Sun and the Planets (page 137)

1. B
2. C
3. A

What Am I?: Jupiter

Earth's Next-Door Neighbors (page 138)

1. Mars (red)
2. Venus (yellow)
3. Mars (red)
4. Venus (yellow)
5. Venus (yellow)
6. Mars (red)

Many, Many Moons (page 139)

1. C
2. B
3. 14 moons should be colored
4. C

Twinkle, Twinkle, Big Star (page 140)

1. star
2. air
3. Earth

Stars with Hair? (page 141)

Three ingredients: ice, dust, rocks

What Do You See in the Stars? (page 142)

1. blue
2. Answers will vary.
3. Answers will vary.

Word Study (page 143)

1. yes
2. no
3. yes
4. no
5. yes

Unit 17

The Third Planet from the Sun (page 144)

Part 1: blue = water; brown = land; white = clouds

Part 2: On Earth, plants produce oxygen. This gas helps create the ozone layer. This layer protects us from the rays of the sun.

A Look Inside Our Planet (page 145)

Part 1:

1. crust
2. mantle
3. outer core
4. inner core

Part 2:

THICK should be written inside the mantle.

LIQUID should be written inside the outer core.

A Puzzle Made of Moving Pieces (page 146)

Part 1: Picture B should be circled.

Part 2: tectonic plates

Our Ever-Changing Earth (page 147)

Section 1: earthquake, volcano

Section 2: Accept reasonable responses.

Section 3: erosion (water running across rock)

All the Days and Years on Earth (page 148)

Part 1: 1. 24 hours; **2.** 365.25 days

What Is in the Air? (page 149)

1. nitrogen
2. oxygen
3. C

Some Facts About Earth (page 150)

Part 1: B

Part 2: name: Mount Everest; continent: Asia; height: 29,000 feet

Word Study (page 151)

Part 1

1. day
2. midnight
3. south
4. inside
5. below

Part 2

1. world
2. 12 p.m.
3. 365 days
4. 24 hours
5. 12 a.m.

Unit 18

Life on a Rocky Planet (page 152)

1. B
2. A
3. C
4. Accept appropriate responses.

The Three Main Kinds of Rock (page 153)

Igneous: 3, 6, 8

Sedimentary: 2, 4, 5

Metamorphic: 1, 7

Answer Key

Rocks That Were Once Liquid (page 154)

Part 1

1. crater
2. lava
3. magma

Part 2:
lava = L, magma = L, rock = S

What Rocks Can Do (page 155)

1. true (brown)
2. false (X)
3. true (brown)
4. false (X)
5. true (brown)
6. true (brown)
7. true (brown)
8. false (X)

Why Soil Is So Important (page 156)
Underground: Students should draw potatoes, carrots, beets, peanuts, or another appropriate plant.

Plants Above Ground: Students should draw a tomato plant, a corn stalk, a lettuce plant, or another appropriate plant.

Fruits on Trees: Students should draw some kind of fruit tree.

All About Sand (page 157)
Part 1: 4, 1, 3, 2
Part 2: $\frac{1}{2}$ mm and 1 mm should be circled.

What's That Ring Made Of? (page 158)

1. gold
2. salt
3. diamond

Word Study (page 159)

M	P	E	B	B	L	E
D	I	R	T	I	N	A
B	O	U	L	D	E	R
E	R	M	U	D	A	T
S	A	N	D	L	S	H

Challenge: minerals

Unit 19

Let's Talk About the Weather (page 160)

1. A
2. B
3. B

What Am I?: meteorologist

Which Season Do You See? (page 161)

1. spring
2. winter
3. summer
4. autumn

Different Places, Different Seasons (page 162)
summer, spring

Today's Rain Has Been Here Before (page 163)

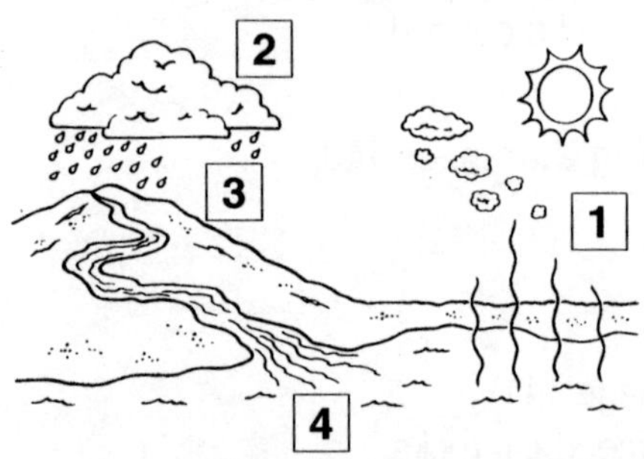

Reading a Weather Forecast (page 164)

1. Monday
2. Thursday
3. Thursday
4. A
5. D

All Kinds of Clouds (page 165)

1. cumulus
2. nimbostratus
3. cirrus

Answer: nimbostratus

Word Study (page 166)
Part 1: torn, a, do
Part 2: hail, rail, rain
Part 3: blowing, bowing, owing, wing, win, in, I